WATERSIDE WALKS

In Devon

Other areas covered in the Waterside Walks series include:

Berkshire
Bristol & Bath
Cheshire
Derbyshire
Devon
Essex
Hampshire
Kent

Lancashire
Lincolnshire
Nottinghamshire
Staffordshire
Suffolk
Surrey
Sussex
Warwickshire
Yorkshire

WATERSIDE WALKS
In Devon

Michael Bennie

COUNTRYSIDE BOOKS
NEWBURY, BERKSHIRE

COUNTRYSIDE BOOKS
3 Catherine Road
Newbury, Berkshire

ISBN 1 85306 557 9

Designed by Graham Whiteman
Cover illustration by Colin Doggett
Maps and photographs by the author

Produced through MRM Associates Ltd., Reading
Typeset by Techniset Typesetters, Newton-le-Willows
Printed by Woolnough Bookbinding Ltd., Irthlingborough

Contents

Introduction   8

Walk

1   Lynmouth Bay and the East Lyn River
(4 miles)   10

2   The Taw Estuary and Braunton Burrows
(8 miles or 6¹/₂ miles)   15

3   The Abbey River and Hartland Quay
(6³/₄ miles)   21

4   The Tarka Trail at Torrington *(6³/₄ miles)*   28

5   The Little Dart River *(3³/₄ miles)*   34

6   The Grand Western Canal *(5 miles)*   40

7   The River Taw at North Tawton *(4 miles)*   45

8   The East Okement Valley *(4¹/₂ miles)*   50

9   The River Otter at Ottery St Mary *(5³/₄ miles)*   57

10   The Teign Gorge *(4 miles)*   63

11   The River Exe and the Exeter Canal *(5 miles)*   68

12   Branscombe and the South Devon Coast
Path *(5 miles)*   74

13   Dawlish Warren: Beach and Estuary
(2¹/₂ miles)   80

14   Dartmoor and the East Dart River *(7¹/₂ miles)*   85

AREA MAP SHOWING LOCATION OF THE WALKS

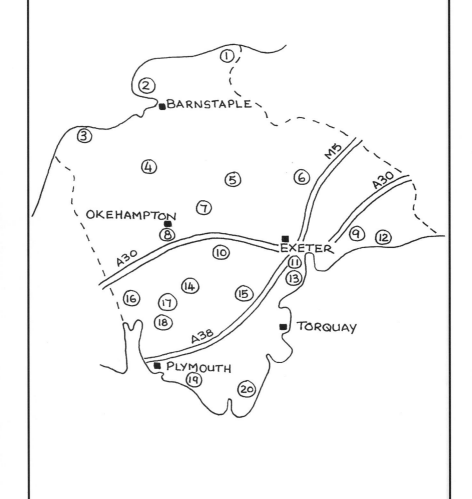

Walk

15   Becky Falls and the River Bovey *(5¹/₂ miles)*   91

16   The Tavy and the Walkham *(5¹/₂ miles)*   96

17   Dartmoor: The Upper Meavy and the
Devonport Leat *(7¹/₂ miles)*   103

18   The Plym and the Lower Meavy *(4¹/₂ miles)*   111

19   The River Avon and Bigbury Bay *(4¹/₂ miles)*   116

20   Hallsands and Start Point *(3³/₄ miles)*   121

PUBLISHER'S NOTE

We hope that you obtain considerable enjoyment from this book; great care has been taken in its preparation. Although at the time of publication all routes followed public rights of way or permitted paths, diversion orders can be made and permissions withdrawn.

We cannot of course be held responsible for such diversion orders and any inaccuracies in the text which result from these or any other changes to the routes nor any damage which might result from walkers trespassing on private property. We are anxious though that all details covering the walks are kept up to date and would therefore welcome information from readers which would be relevant to future editions.

INTRODUCTION

The landscape of Devon is one of the most varied of any county in England. It includes rugged, rocky coasts, long, sandy beaches, barren moorland, rolling hills, thickly wooded valleys, rich farm fields and lush, green meadows, all in abundance. And wherever you are in the county, you are seldom far from water of some kind, be it a chattering stream, a raging torrent, a placid canal, a majestic river estuary or the pounding waves of the sea.

This collection of walks takes you on some of the most attractive routes along the waterways or coasts of Devon. It explores the county's cliffs, beaches, streams, rivers, canals — even a leat — and stretches from the north coast to the south, from the wild wastes of Dartmoor to the woods and fields of East Devon. There is a brief description of the background to each walk and what you are likely to encounter en route, as well as information on suitable places to stop for a meal or a drink — sometimes a tearoom, more often a pub. This is followed by advice on getting to the start of the walk and parking, and then a detailed description of the route itself. In case you want a longer outing, I have also given suggestions for places you may like to visit in the vicinity of each walk.

Sketch maps are provided, but it must be emphasised that these are for guidance only. For navigational purposes I would suggest using the appropriate Ordnance Survey map, details of which are given in the walk descriptions. I find that the best maps for walking are the ones on a scale of 1:25,000 — either the Outdoor Leisure or the new Explorer series — as these give more detail than the Landranger 1:50,000 maps, including such things as field boundaries, which can be very useful in working out where you are. Between them these two series now cover the whole of Devon, and I strongly recommend them. There is just one word of warning on the Explorer series. Two of the maps I refer to, Exmouth and Sidmouth and Torquay and Dawlish, are due to be renumbered as the series progresses. At present they are numbered 30 and 31 respectively, but they are due to become 115 and 110 respectively. You therefore need to ensure that you have the right one by checking the title as well as the number. I have given both numbers in the route descriptions.

Most of the walks are around 5 miles or less, although there are a few that are longer (the longest is 8 miles, but there is a short cut for those who do not want to do the full distance), and they cover a wide variety of terrain. They are all well within the scope of an averagely fit person, but it has to be borne in mind that Devon is a hilly county, and the ground can also sometimes be a bit rough, especially on the moor or along the coast. However, where there may be particular problems — a steep climb, a muddy path or rough ground — it is mentioned in the route summary. Stout shoes or even trainers are quite suitable for most of the routes in dry weather, but do remember that where there is water there is often mud, so walking boots or wellingtons may be better when there has been rain.

I hope you get as much pleasure from exploring these routes as I did — happy walking!

Michael Bennie

LYNMOUTH BAY AND THE EAST LYN RIVER

This is one of the most beautiful walks in the county, taking in both the rugged North Devon coastline and the lovely wooded valley of the East Lyn River. There are some magnificent views to enjoy along the way and the pretty village of Lynmouth to explore at the start or finish. There are a few steady climbs on the Coast Path, but nothing too strenuous.

The East Lyn River.

Not for nothing was the area around Lynmouth and Lynton known to the Victorians as 'Little Switzerland'. Its stunning scenery and quiet charm have ensured that it remains popular with holidaymakers, and it is a walkers' delight.

This walk starts in the lovely village of Lynmouth. Devastated by the flooding of both the East and West Lyn Rivers in 1952, which resulted in the loss of 93 buildings and 31 lives, enough remains or has been restored to make it one of the prettiest coastal villages in Devon. A unique feature is the water-operated cliff railway, which links it with its twin, Lynton.

From there, we follow the South-West Coast Path round Lynmouth Bay, with some very good views up and down the coast, before turning inland across farm fields, with a superb panorama of Exmoor to accompany us. We then descend into the wooded valley of the East Lyn River to Watersmeet House. This Victorian fishing lodge, which sits at the confluence of the East Lyn and Hoar Oak Water, is now owned by the National Trust, and is operated by them as a restaurant, tea garden and shop (telephone: 01598 753348). It serves coffee, home-made light lunches and cream teas in an idyllic setting, but is unfortunately only open between the end of March and the end of October. The route then follows the picturesque valley of the East Lyn back to Lynmouth.

In addition to Watersmeet House, I can recommend the Rock House Hotel (telephone: 01598 753508) for refreshments. It is a delightful thatched establishment between the river and the sea in Lynmouth, and offers teas, coffees and a range of bar meals.

- **HOW TO GET THERE:** Lynmouth is on the A39 between Barnstaple and Minehead.
- **PARKING:** There are three car parks in Lynmouth, all of which are convenient for the start of the walk. Two are just off the A39, to the south of the river, and the third is at the bottom of the village, beyond the harbour.
- **LENGTH OF THE WALK:** 4 miles. Maps: OS Landranger 180 Barnstaple and Ilfracombe; OS Outdoor Leisure 9 Exmoor (GR 722495).

THE WALK

1. If you have parked beyond the harbour, return along Riverside Road until you come to a footbridge across the river on your left. If you have parked on the opposite side of the A39, then cross the road and follow Riverside Road down to the footbridge. Cross the bridge and you will see the Rock House Hotel on your left. Follow the path round to the right into a park and then to the left of a putting green.

The tarred path skirts the park and continues along the foreshore before turning right beyond a private garden. Follow it round and

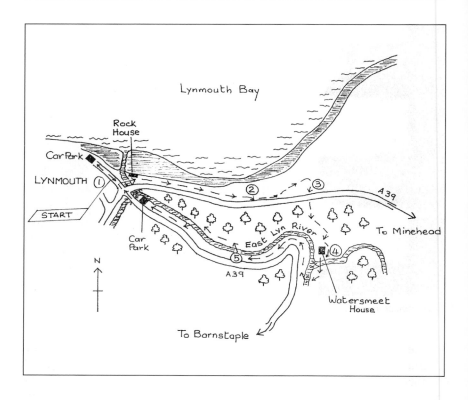

then after a few yards leave it, following the Coast Path sign to your left. You go up some steps into a very pretty wood, carpeted with wild flowers. It is particularly lovely in the spring, with the blue of the bluebells intermingled with the white of the three-cornered leeks.

After a short climb, follow the Coast Path sign to the left again, between a wall and a high bank. The path continues to climb steadily but not too steeply, with the sea visible on the left over the wall. It zigzags up the slope, still climbing steadily, and comes out onto the A39.

2. Follow the path on the bank alongside the road, with a very steep slope down to the sea on your left dotted with rhododendrons. After about 250 yards you come to a pull-in with a National Trust sign for the Foreland at the end. Turn left off the road immediately beyond it.

Watersmeet House.

The path runs along the side of the slope, with a view along Lynmouth Bay ahead. The path winds and climbs along the edge of a hillside covered in gorse and bracken dotted with heather and bilberries. After about $3/4$ mile, you cross a stile and the path runs just below a field. At this point you get a lovely view back along the coast to Lynmouth, with Lynton above it. At the end of the field the path goes to the right and you come to a junction; go right (signposted to Watersmeet) to a gate.

3. Bear left along the side of the field on the other side and go down some steps to another gate, leading onto the A39. Cross the road to another gate. Go down the hill on the other side, following the sign to Watersmeet, not the one to Lynmouth. Go round a small dam and to the right, still following the Watersmeet sign.

The path now runs along the top of a valley and you get a superb view ahead of you, over woods and farms. Soon you will see the East Lyn River cascading down through the woods below you. After about 500 yards you cross a stile, go down some steps and follow the path as it skirts the top of a wood. You come to a junction; turn right (signposted to Watersmeet again).

This path runs along the top of the ridge, with the wood falling away on either side. At the end of the ridge it begins to descend into the wood, which along here is carpeted with bilberries. It twists and turns as it goes down, and you get an occasional glimpse of the river below you. Near the bottom, you come to another junction; turn right and you will come out at Watersmeet House.

4. If you are not stopping for refreshments here, go past the house and cross a footbridge on the left and then cross another one. Turn right on the other side to follow the left bank of the river. The path joins a track by a bridge; follow it alongside the river, and when the track climbs up the hill turn off onto a clear path (signposted to Lynmouth). The path turns left away from the river briefly to bypass a private house, then crosses a drive and rejoins the river on the other side. This is a gorgeous stretch along the bottom of a steep-sided wooded valley, with the river bubbling and churning over a series of rocks and rapids beside you.

You pass a footbridge and the path climbs up to the road before veering back down to the river again.

5. You come to another footbridge; cross over onto the right bank and follow the often flower-lined path downstream. At the next footbridge, cross over again and continue down on the left bank again. Where the path forks on the outskirts of Lynmouth, go right. Climb some steps alongside another footbridge and you will soon find the car park on your left. If you have parked at the bottom of the village, continue to the main road, cross over and follow Riverside Road back past the harbour.

PLACES OF INTEREST

In Lynmouth you can visit the *Woodside Craft Centre* and the *Exmoor Brass Rubbing Centre*. Up the hill in Lynton you will find the *Lyn and Exmoor Museum*, which has displays of the tools and work of local craftsmen. Just the other side of Lynton is the *Valley of Rocks*, a fascinating area of rocks which have weathered into the strangest forms.

WALK 2

THE TAW ESTUARY AND BRAUNTON BURROWS

Variety is the keynote of this fairly long but undemanding route. It combines beautiful stretches of riverside and coastal walking with areas of considerable natural and historical interest, including one of the largest sand dune systems in the country and one of the few remaining examples of the open-field system of cultivation which was a feature of medieval England. It is all along easy paths and lanes and there is virtually no climbing.

The River Caen at Braunton.

Braunton is well known amongst naturalists and conservationists as the home of Braunton Burrows, a national nature reserve which comprises one of the largest sand dune systems in Britain – over 4 square miles of them running inland from the magnificent 4-mile beach of Saunton Sands. The reserve contains over 400 species of flowering plants and a wide variety of mammals and birds.

15

Of interest to historians is Braunton Great Field, on the edge of the town, one of the last remaining examples of the system of open-field cultivation which was prevalent across much of lowland England during the Middle Ages. Under this system fields were cultivated in strips, with no hedges, walls or fences to separate them. Farmers co-operated by agreeing which crops would be planted in each field and which fields should be left fallow, and by sharing the labour. Although the vast majority of open-field systems were either gradually privatised by agreement or abolished by the Enclosure Acts of the 18th and 19th centuries, Braunton Great Field looks very much as it must have done in its heyday. The main change is that whereas there would once have been 100 farmers working it, there are now just five.

This undemanding walk leads you across both these sites, taking in two rivers along the way and with the opportunity to explore the vast expanse of Saunton Sands as well as Braunton Burrows. You follow the River Caen down to where it joins the Taw, passing Velator Quay, another site of interest, as you go. The quay was used from early in the 19th century for the shipment of local produce, but began to decline after the coming of the railway at the end of the century and is now used only by pleasure craft.

You then swing round to follow the Taw to the coast and make your way through Braunton Burrows to Saunton Sands (or, if you want a shorter route, take an inland track to skirt the reserve). The return leg takes you along country lanes and across Braunton Great Field.

There are several pubs, restaurants and cafés in Braunton, but the most convenient for this walk is the London Inn (telephone: 01271 812603), a homely hostelry next to the car park, which has a good array of fare from snacks to main meals.

- **HOW TO GET THERE:** Braunton is on the A361 between Barnstaple and Ilfracombe.
- **PARKING:** There is a free car park in the centre of Braunton. Turn west off the A361 onto the B3231 towards Croyde and you will see it signposted on your left.
- **LENGTH OF THE WALK:** 8 miles (full route); 6½ miles (shorter route skirting Braunton Burrows and missing out Saunton Sands). Maps: OS Landranger 180 Barnstaple and Ilfracombe; OS Explorer 139 Bideford, Ilfracombe and Barnstaple (GR 487365).

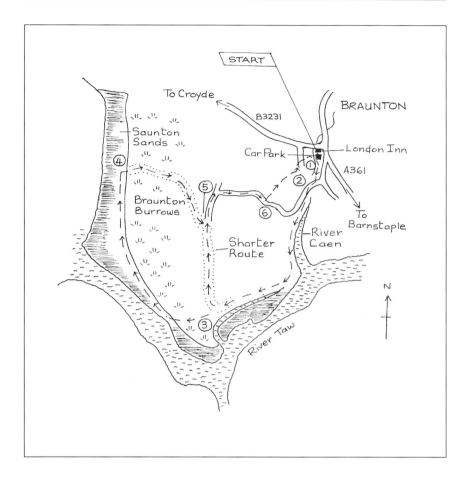

THE WALK

1. Start from the overflow area of the car park; turn left along the surfaced path which runs beside the River Caen. Where the path forks at the end, go left (signposted to the Burrows and Barnstaple), and then right along the road, still following the same sign. After about 100 yards turn right off the road (still signposted to the Burrows and Barnstaple) onto a broad track. Follow it round to the left and you will soon find yourself alongside the river again.

2. The track emerges onto a road; turn right. After about 150 yards, you will see a Coast Path sign pointing left. Leave the road here,

17

cross a small rivulet and bear right to follow the bank of the river downstream. After another 300 yards or so, you pass Velator Quay and cross a stone stile. Continue to follow the path along the bank above the slow flowing river. Cross another wall via a stone stile, and then a fence via a wooden one, and continue to follow the bank as it curves left alongside the river, away from the road you have been tracking on the right.

Cross yet another stile, after which the Caen joins the River Taw and the path swings round to the right to follow the latter downstream. Up ahead of you, on the other side of the river, you can now see Appledore, and you get a very good view up the Taw to your left. This is a lovely, peaceful stretch which runs straight as a die for about $^3/_4$ mile.

At the end, you will see a white house on your right. Cross a stile alongside it, and just beyond it go down some steps and turn right up a track. After a few yards, at the road, turn left. The road deteriorates to a broad track and you pass a large parking area on your left and then enter the Braunton Burrows Nature Reserve.

3. You pass another parking area and the track turns right. Here you have a choice: you can go straight on along a boardwalk to walk among the dunes to the beach; or you can turn right and follow the track as it skirts the nature reserve, up to the lane alongside the car park in point 5, saving about $1^1/_2$ miles but missing the abundance of flowers, rabbits, foxes and other wildlife which have made the burrows their home.

If you decide to go through the reserve, follow the boardwalk as it winds and climbs among the dunes, and after about $^1/_2$ mile you will come out onto the beach of Saunton Sands; turn right. After following the beach for about a mile, you will come to two sandy tracks running up into the dunes. Ignore these and continue for another $1^1/_4$ miles or so until you see another track leading away from the beach and into the reserve.

4. Turn right here and follow the track as it winds in amongst the dunes for about $1^1/_4$ miles. Ignore any turn-offs to the right or left, keeping to the main track all the way to a car park.

5. Turn left beyond the car park into a lane. (If you have followed the track to skirt the reserve, it will bring you out at the lane

Velator Quay.

alongside the car park after about 1½ miles.) Follow the lane for about 500 yards and at the first junction you come to, turn right. After a long, straight stretch, this second lane curves to the left and then takes a sharp turn to the right. Follow it round.

6. When it next turns to the right, however, branch off left across a stile next to a gate, following the yellow waymark. Turn right alongside the hedge, and when that goes off to the right, carry straight on across the field.

This is Braunton Great Field, which is fascinating to walk across because of its complete lack of hedges or field boundaries of any kind – the crops are divided by little more than paths and narrow tracks. The path across the field brings you out at a track; bear right. When it joins another one, go straight on, and at the next junction straight on again. You then come to a T-junction; turn right and follow the new track round to the left. At the end of the Great Field, turn left along a track until it joins a road. Follow the road for about 150 yards until you see a public footpath sign pointing right between the houses. Go down this path and at the end turn left alongside the river. After a few yards turn right

Braunton Burrows.

across a bridge and then almost immediately left into the car park.

PLACES OF INTEREST
Ashford Gardens, 3 miles away towards Barnstaple, has 2 acres of landscaped gardens, an adventure playground and an exotic butterfly house. Some 5 miles in the other direction, in Croyde, you will find *Cascades*, a family adventure pool, and the *Gem Rock and Shell Museum*. At Woolacombe (9 miles) there is *Once Upon a Time*, a children's theme park.

WALK 3

THE ABBEY RIVER AND HARTLAND QUAY

This interesting ramble follows the picturesque valley of the Abbey River, sometimes alongside the water, sometimes higher up the hillside, down to the spectacular cliffs and coves of the North Devon coast. There are a couple of historical sites to visit along the way, and the return journey follows lanes and woodland paths back along the valley. There is one steep climb along the coast, but otherwise the route is fairly easy.

The mouth of the Abbey River.

The Hartland area is full of historical interest, as well as being a beautiful spot to explore. St Nectan, a Welsh missionary, was murdered here in the 6th century, and his memory still dominates the area: both the Roman Catholic and Church of England churches in Hartland are dedicated to him, as is the church in the neighbouring village of Stoke (which also has a well named after him), and the ruins of his monastery are in the grounds of the more recent abbey just to the west of Hartland itself.

This abbey, which you pass along the way, was founded in the 12th century as an Augustinian establishment, but became a private residence with the dissolution of the monasteries in the 16th century. It is open to the public on Wednesday, Thursday and Sunday afternoons from May to September, also on Tuesdays in July and August, and on bank holidays and at Easter.

Halfway round the route, you can walk down to Hartland Quay. There was a harbour here until the end of the 19th century, mainly used for the export of malt and corn and the import of lime, sand and gravel, but it was destroyed by gales (not for the first time). Because of the contemporary improvements in road and rail transport, it was uneconomic to repair it again, and it fell into disuse. Its history is recorded in an interesting little museum at the quay, which also contains many other nautical artefacts, mainly concerned with the many shipwrecks along this stretch of coast.

Also at Hartland Quay is the Hartland Quay Hotel (telephone: 01237 441218), an attractive inn with good views over the sea from the terrace outside and a homely atmosphere inside. It serves a range of bar snacks, meals and daily specials, and there is a shop attached selling ice creams and gifts.

The walk starts in Hartland itself, now little more than a large village but a major centre in Elizabethan times, more important than Bideford. If you are looking for refreshment before or after your walk rather than in the middle, there are three pubs and a café in Hartland itself. My recommendation is the Hart Inn, just by the car park (telephone: 01237 441474), a pleasant hostelry with a 'local' feel, which has a beer garden in which you can sample their real ales and home-made fare.

The route follows the Abbey River – sometimes alongside it, sometimes up on the hillside above – down to its mouth, and then turns south along the cliff top, with a spectacular view along the coast. It is worth the extra effort to walk down to Hartland Quay, and back and then you return along the opposite side of the river valley. In addition to this magnificent coastal stretch, the route includes delightful woods, pretty farm paths and quiet lanes.

- **HOW TO GET THERE:** The B3248, which turns north off the A39 between Bideford and Bude, takes you straight to Hartland.
- **PARKING:** There is a car park just off the main street.
- **LENGTH OF THE WALK:** 6 $^3/_4$ miles. Maps: OS Landranger 190 Bude, Clovelly and surrounding area; OS Explorer 126 Clovelly and Hartland (GR 259245).

THE WALK

1. Leave the car park via the vehicle entrance. You will find the Hart Inn on your right as you do so. Turn left and go down to the main street of the village; turn left again and you will pass the Anchor Inn on your right. Turn left just beyond it, into School Lane. At the T-junction, turn left and at the next junction go right (signposted to Ball Hill). This lane takes you out of the village and down a steep hill past some houses. At the junction bear right (signposted to Hartland Point and the lighthouse).

2. Cross over the Abbey River and at the junction on the other side, turn left. When the lane curves right up a hill, leave it to bear left, following the public footpath sign. The path leads into a pretty wood, alongside the river. Cross a stile and continue along the right-hand side of a meadow, with the river on the other side of it. Where the path forks towards the end of the meadow, take the broad track which goes left alongside the river for a short while again.

At the end, cross a stile onto a track. After a few yards turn right, following the footpath sign, to climb up through the wood. You emerge via a stile into a field; keep to the right, alongside a hedge. Pause at the top for a magnificent view back across farms and woods, and left across to Stoke church, with its tall tower, and beyond.

Cross a stile onto a track and turn left. There is another very good view across Stoke church to the sea ahead and, in summer, a superb display of flowers on either side of you. After a while the track enters a wood and begins to descend. It bends to the left between high banks and eventually emerges onto a lane just opposite the gate to Hartland Abbey. If you are not visiting the house and gardens, turn right and follow the lane as it climbs up through the wood.

3. After about 500 yards, look out for a public footpath sign half

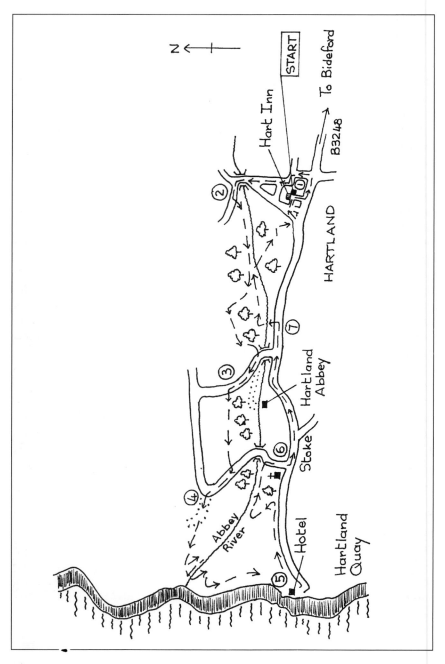

hidden in the hedge on your left. Go through a gate and bear right towards a stile which looks rather odd standing all alone in the middle of the field – presumably there was once a fence on either side of it. Go past it and you now get a superb view to the left and ahead. On the horizon you can see the ruin of what is presumed to have been a summer house belonging to the abbey standing out rather spectacularly against the sky.

Cross a stile (this time with a fence) and keep to the top of the next field to reach two stiles in quick succession. Keep to the right again to reach a gate leading onto a lane. Turn right and follow the lane through a farm.

4. When the lane turns sharp right beyond it, turn left across a stile, following the public footpath sign. Follow the track on the other side; as you go you will see the sea across the bank ahead of you. Go through a gate and continue along the track beyond, following the right-hand edge of a field. Just as it turns to the right to follow the wall round, you will see another track, less well defined but still quite clear, leading off to the left; follow that. It soon becomes a grassy path and then after about 100 yards crosses a low bank. Turn sharp left and follow a somewhat overgrown path between banks down towards the valley, crossing a stile along the way.

At the bottom it joins a track; turn sharp right and just before a white cottage turn left, following the Coast Path sign. Go through a kissing gate and across a field. Turn right, following the waymark, to cross a bridge over the Abbey River and then a stile. At the path junction, go right through a gate, still following the Coast Path sign. The path now climbs up to the cliff top. It is a steep climb, but fairly short, and at the top you are rewarded with a spectacular view south along the coast.

5. You pass the ruin you saw on the horizon earlier. To visit Hartland Quay, go to the right of the cottage you can see ahead of you to a stile. Turn right, following the Coast Path sign, along a roughly surfaced track, to join a road, which goes round to the right and then to the left to the quay and the hotel. To return to the main route, retrace your steps up the road, and just beyond the cottage at the top, go left through a gate, following the public footpath sign, and turn immediately right alongside a bank.

If you do not want to visit the quay, go to the left of the cottage

Stoke church.

as you come along the coast to where you can see the footpath sign up against the bank, and turn left when you reach it. Cross a stone stile at the end of the field and keep to the right of the next field. At the end turn left and follow the edge of the field down into the valley. At the bottom you come to a path junction; turn right down some steps into another pretty wood, just above the river. Go through two gates into a meadow and cross to another gate leading into a lane. Turn right and follow the lane as it climbs and winds up to the village of Stoke.

6. At the T-junction by the church, turn left. At the next junction, go straight on (signposted to Hartland and Bideford). The lane takes you into a wood, and you will find the river on your left once again, with the grounds of Hartland Abbey beyond it. At the next junction go straight on again (again signposted to Hartland and Bideford).

7. About $^3/_4$ mile after leaving Stoke you will come to a house called Hartland Mill; turn left here down a track, following the public footpath sign to Hartland. You cross the river and at the track junction turn sharp right. You will find a dense wood above you on the left and the river on the other side of an often flower-filled meadow on the right. You pass the path you took to climb out of the wood on the outward journey, and cross the stile beyond. Instead of going straight ahead on the other side, however, turn right to go down to the river and across a footbridge.

Bear left on the other side, along a broad path through the wood. It widens into a track and then narrows again as it skirts the edge of the wood, with Hartland Observatory on the left. At the top go round to the left to a kissing gate leading onto a road. Turn right and at the T-junction go left into West Street. Where the main road turns left, go straight on, past the Hart Inn, to the car park.

PLACES OF INTEREST

In addition to *Hartland Quay* and *Hartland Abbey*, which are passed on the walk, you can visit *The Milky Way and North Devon Bird of Prey Centre*, 3 miles away off the A39. This multi-faceted attraction includes a farm park, falconry displays, slides, rides and other children's activities.

WALK 4

THE TARKA TRAIL AT TORRINGTON

This picturesque walk follows part of the Tarka Trail, the long-distance route which covers much of the countryside in which the classic 'Tarka the Otter' was set. We take it in two bites, one along a tributary of the River Torridge and the other criss-crossing the Torridge itself, separated by farm paths and lanes with some lovely views. Much of the walking is through woodland, with some pretty farmland in between.

The River Torridge seen from the Tarka Trail.

The Rivers Taw and Torridge and their tributaries were the setting for Henry Williamson's popular evocation of river life, *Tarka the Otter*. A long-distance route, the Tarka Trail, has been devised which takes in many of the places associated with Tarka's exploits, stretching from Dartmoor to the coast at Barnstaple.

Starting at the old railway station just outside Great Torrington, this route follows part of that trail along a disused railway line as it winds alongside a tributary of the Torridge, the Langtree Lake. This stretch is beautifully wooded and because the path follows the railway line, the going is very easy. It then cuts up across farm fields and quiet lanes, with some extensive views across the rolling hills of North Devon, before rejoining the Tarka Trail lower down the disused railway, on the banks of the Torridge itself. It then crosses and recrosses the river as the latter meanders slowly towards the sea in a series of loops.

If you are in need of refreshment, the Puffing Billy (telephone: 01805 623050), at the start of the walk, was the old station building. It now offers a variety of bar snacks, as well as cream teas, and has a pleasant garden. Alternatively, a short detour of 200 yards or so in the middle of the walk will bring you to the Clinton Arms at Frithelstock (telephone: 01805 623279), a pretty inn with tables out on the village green, which serves a wide range of snacks and restaurant meals in a lovely setting.

- **HOW TO GET THERE:** The walk starts alongside the Tarka Trail at the Puffing Billy just north of Great Torrington on the A386 Okehampton to Bideford road.
- **PARKING:** There is public parking by the pub. Do make sure that you go to the right parking area, however. There is a car park just down the road on the outskirts of Great Torrington itself, with toilets and a picnic area. That is not the one you want. You should look for the Tarka Trail and Puffing Billy signs, further out of the town beyond the derestriction signs.
- **LENGTH OF THE WALK:** 6³/₄ miles. Maps: OS Landranger 180 Barnstaple and Ilfracombe; OS Explorer 126 Clovelly and Hartland (GR 480197).

THE WALK

1. Walk down the driveway towards the disused railway and turn right to pass under the road. This is the Tarka Trail. After a few yards you cross a bridge high above the Torridge, with lovely views of the river on both sides. The bridge then crosses the smaller Langtree Lake, and the track goes to the right. You cross a farm track and enter a beautiful wooded area, with the river down below on your right.

Go through a gate, ignoring the public bridleway signs on either side, and continue along the main track, with the river immediately below you down a bank on the right. It is a lovely area, with the

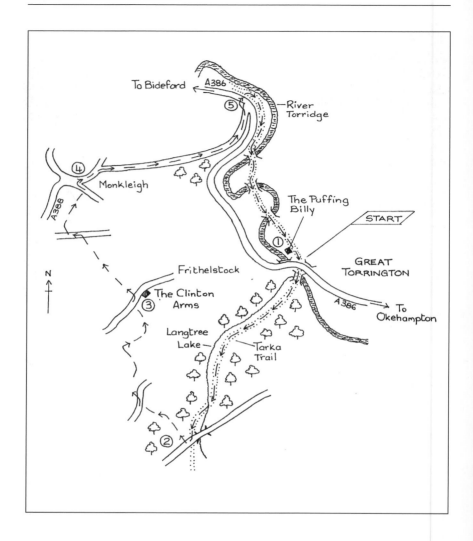

woods full of birdsong and a variety of wild flowers lining the track in their season. The river meanders along through the undergrowth on the right, sometimes alongside the track, sometimes further away, but never out of earshot.

After about 1½ miles the track crosses the river and continues for about 200 yards on the other bank until it meets a road. This is where you leave the Tarka Trail temporarily; go through a gate onto the road and turn right.

Beam Weir on the River Torridge.

2. You pass a track on your right, and a few yards beyond it turn right, following the public footpath sign. The path climbs into a wood. Go through a gate and continue along the path as it skirts the wood, with a field on the right. Where the path forks, take the right-hand fork and climb up a slope to the top of a rise. When you come to a hedge, go through a gateway, keeping the hedge on your left. Cross the field to a gate and cross the next field to another gate, leading onto a track. Turn left and go through yet another gate. Follow the track past the farm buildings and then round to the right.

It comes out onto a lane; turn right. After about 150 yards, as the lane curves to the right, go left through a gate, following the public footpath sign. Follow the track on the other side, and when it turns left, bear right along the edge of the field, following the yellow waymark. You get a very good view over the undulating farmland to the right as you go. At the end of the field, turn left down a track, still following the yellow waymark. The track goes to the right and you pass through a gate. Continue along the track on the other side, and when it peters out continue along the edge of the field. At the end turn right to follow the hedge round, and again you get a lovely view.

After following the hedge for about 300 yards, you will come across a waymarked stile on your left. Cross it and make your way straight across the field beyond, aiming a little to the left of the house you can see ahead of you. As you come over the brow of the hill, you will see a cottage at the bottom; aim for that and go through a gate to the right of it onto a road.

3. Turn right and just beyond the farm buildings on the left, you will see a public footpath sign pointing left across a cattle grid. Turn off the road here. If you want to stop at the Clinton Arms, however, go straight on for about 200 yards and you will find it on your right.

Having turned off the road, go through a gate and keep to the right of the field beyond. Go through the gate in the corner ahead and follow the hedge down the field, with more good views all around. You cross a wooden barrier at the bottom, and then have to negotiate a rather dilapidated gate – it may be better to go round it, as the last time I was there it was almost impossible to open. Cross a stream and go up the field on the other side towards two gates; go through the left-hand one and keep to the right of the next field. Go through a gate at the end onto a lane and turn left.

Follow the lane for about 150 yards to a public footpath sign pointing through a gate on the right. Cross a field to another gate, and as you do so you get what is probably the best view yet over to the right. Bear right beyond the gate, aiming for the corner of a hedge. Cross a stile and bear left across the next field to a gate. Bear right on the other side, following a grassy track to another gate leading onto a track. Follow the track up to a road and bear left into Monkleigh.

4. At the junction, turn right (signposted to Weare Giffard) and at the next junction follow the main lane round to the right (signposted to Weare Giffard again). This is a lovely quiet, hedge-fringed lane, with a good view up ahead and Great Torrington half right. It skirts the edge of a wood after a while, and after about $1^1/_2$ miles joins the A386.

5. Just before it does so, branch off to the left, following the Tarka Trail sign, to go under the main road. On the other side bear left up some steps to rejoin the trail; turn right. This is a lovely wooded track, which again follows the disused railway as it crosses and recrosses the River Torridge. Continue along it for about a mile to the Puffing Billy and the car park. To reach the latter, you need to continue along the trail to the left of the pub and turn right beyond it.

PLACES OF INTEREST

The *Dartington Crystal* works at Great Torrington are worth a visit. They are open to the public, and offer guided tours, during which you can watch the craftsmen blowing and shaping the glass. A mile beyond Great Torrington is the Royal Horticultural Society's *Rosemoor Garden*, 40 acres of beautiful and varied gardens, including 2,000 roses. And at Merton (9 miles south), you will find *Barometer World*, with displays of barometers stretching back 300 years.

THE LITTLE DART RIVER

The valley of the Little Dart is one of the most delightfully unspoilt areas of mid-Devon, and this undemanding route explores a particularly pretty stretch of it. It is a very varied walk, taking in woods and fields, farm paths and hedge-fringed green lanes full of wildlife – in addition, of course, to the river itself. There are one or two muddy patches, so stout shoes or boots are recommended.

The Little Dart River.

Mid-Devon is a fertile area of lush, green farmland and attractive wooded valleys, and this lovely walk takes in a bit of both. It passes along the valley of the Little Dart, a tributary of the River Taw, before following tiny streams up through the woods to explore the fields, paths and green lanes of the farmland above.

It starts at the small village of Chawleigh, which boasts some very pretty cottages and other buildings alongside the less appealing modern housing which straddles the main road. The area around the church and school is particularly attractive. Surprisingly, considering its size, it boasts two pubs, both very pleasant hostelries: the Royal Oak (telephone: 01769 580427) towards the north-western end of the village and the Earl of Portsmouth (telephone: 01769 580204) in the centre. The route description starts at the latter. It has an attractive eating area and a beer garden, and it serves a wide variety of food, from soup and bar snacks to vegetarian dishes and grills; its speciality, however, is steaks.

- **HOW TO GET THERE:** Chawleigh is on the B3042, 2 miles east of the A377 Exeter to Barnstaple road, and is signposted from the latter.
- **PARKING:** There is parking along the main road, and in some of the side roads. But do park with consideration for others, and do not block entrances or cause bottlenecks.
- **LENGTH OF THE WALK:** $3\,^3/_4$ miles. Maps: OS Landranger 180 Barnstaple and Ilfracombe; OS Explorer 127 South Molton and Chulmleigh (GR 711125).

THE WALK

1. From the main road turn east past the Earl of Portsmouth (signposted to Cheldon and Gidley Arms). This lane takes you down a hill and out of the village. It continues to descend between high hedges into the valley of the Little Dart. After nearly $^3/_4$ mile, it crosses the river.

At the road junction immediately on the other side, turn right (signposted to Cheldon). Follow this attractive, hedge-fringed lane for about $^1/_4$ mile to another junction. Here, instead of following the main lane round to the left, go straight on (signposted to Lapford). Cross a small stone bridge.

2. Immediately beyond the bridge you will see a public footpath sign and a stile on your left; cross the stile into a field and you will find the Little Dart on your right. Keep to the bank of the river as you go through this long, narrow field. It is a lovely path, with the placid, tree-lined river on your right and a wood climbing the hill on the other side of the field on your left.

At the end of the field, you cross a stile into a wood. This is another pretty stretch, with the sun filtering through the trees and dappling the river as it flows over the rocks alongside you. Before

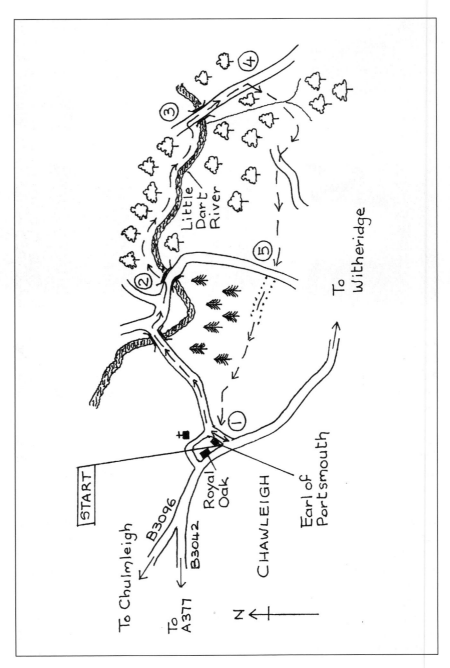

START

To Chulmleigh

B3096

To A377

B3042

Royal Oak

CHAWLEIGH

Earl of Portsmouth

N

To Witheridge

Little Dart River

The Earl of Portsmouth pub, Chawleigh.

long, however, you leave the wood via yet another stile; cross the field beyond to a gap in the middle of a hedge and cross the next field to a stile, still with the river on your right. Beyond the stile is a piece of waste ground; make your way through the bracken until the path emerges onto a lane.

3. Turn right and cross the river again. The lane climbs steadily through a wood on the other side. After a while it emerges from the wood and continues to climb – a little less steeply now – between hedges.

4. About 600 yards from the bridge, you will come to a gap in the hedge on the right – there is a public footpath sign, but it is on the left, and is obscured by the hedge. Turn right here and keep to the right of the line of brambles, gorse and bracken which form a kind of barrier across the field beyond. At the end you will come to a wood; follow the clear path which runs into it.

Soon the path broadens into a track running between high banks and starts to go down into a valley. You pass another track going off to the right; keep going straight on. At the bottom you will find a

37

The lych gate at Chawleigh church.

muddy patch; bear right to cross a stream and you will find another muddy patch on the other side. Navigate your way around it, and you will find that the track becomes drier. It climbs through the wood, with a stream chattering away on the left, and then curves to the right and eventually leaves the wood.

Go through a gate at the end and turn left into a lane through a farm. After about 100 yards, as the lane curves left, go straight on up a track. When the track turns right, go straight on through a gate, following the public footpath sign. Cross a field to a gate, then another field to a gap in a hedge (you have to duck under some wooden bars to go through it). The views along here are very good, especially to the right.

Cross two more fields separated by another gate and you will come to a third gate. Go through that onto a piece of waste ground. The path takes you parallel to the right-hand hedge and then curves round to the right, to lead you between two hedges. It comes out at a track, which leads you to a lane.

5. Turn left and then almost immediately right along a track, following a public footpath sign. The track becomes a green lane lined with hedges and full of birds and flowers in summer. After 600 yards it ends at a gate leading into a field. You will see the tower of Chawleigh church ahead of you. Aim slightly to the left of that as you cross the field. When you get to the other side, you will see a yellow waymark pointing through a gap in the bank and trees to a stile.

Cross the stile and follow the path as it descends quite steeply through bracken and gorse on the other side. At the bottom, you enter a wood; go right and then left, again following the yellow arrows, and cross a small stream followed by a stile. Take the path up through the wood on the other side and you will emerge into a field. Keep to the left and at the top you will find a large gap in the hedge on your left. Go through it to a stile and follow the track on the other side. This brings you out at a lane; turn left and you will soon see the Earl of Portsmouth on your right.

PLACES OF INTEREST

About 2¹/₂ miles south-west of Chawleigh, just across the A377, is *Eggesford Gardens*, a combined garden centre and country park. At Winkleigh (7 miles south-west) you will find the *Square Gallery*, a fine collection of paintings, sculptures, jewellery and other arts and crafts. And the *Down St Mary Vineyard*, about 8 miles away, off the A377 to the south, offers a chance to sample some of their wines.

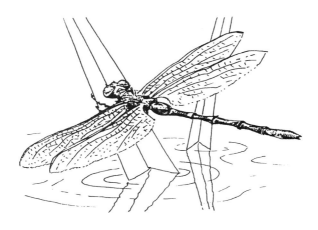

WALK 6

THE GRAND WESTERN CANAL

On this route, a beautiful, peaceful amble alongside the Grand Western Canal is followed by a stretch along quiet country lanes and a visit to the attractive village of Halberton before you rejoin the canal for the final leg. It is a very easy walk, and apart from the attractions of the canal and its wildlife there are some very pretty views along the way.

The village pond, Halberton.

As its name suggests, the Grand Western Canal was originally intended to be somewhat more extensive than the small local waterway we see today. The ambitious ideas of the planners included: providing a route from the Somerset ports to Exeter to avoid the South Wales coal having to be brought round via Land's End; linking Bristol and the English Channel; and even making the canal part of a much longer waterway which would connect London with Exeter.

The first 11 miles of the canal, from Tiverton to the Somerset border, were built between 1810 and 1814, and 20 years later it was extended to Taunton, but that is where construction ended and the more grandiose schemes came to nothing. Indeed, even the newer section was not used for very long – it was closed in 1867. The original stretch continued in use, but it fell into decline after the 1920s. It was revived in the 1960s, and is now designated by the county council as a country park.

We follow just under 3 miles of the canal between Tiverton and the attractive little village of Halberton in two sections, split by a lovely stretch along quiet country lanes. The canal is alive with waterfowl and other wildlife, and the banks are fringed with wild flowers in the spring and summer. There are good views across the undulating farmland of mid-Devon, especially when you get into the lanes higher up the valley. In Halberton, a short detour of about 300 yards will bring you to the Barge (telephone: 01884 820316), a friendly pub where you can be sure of a warm welcome and a good variety of food and drink, including the usual bar snacks and 'specials' which might range from curry and tagliatelli to soup and fish dishes.

- **HOW TO GET THERE:** The walk starts where the Tiverton to Halberton road crosses the Grand Western Canal. Approaching on the M5, leave at junction 27 and follow the A361 towards Tiverton. Take the first turning to the left off this road (signposted to Sampford Peverell and Halberton) and go through both villages, following the signs to Tiverton. The crossing is about $1/2$ mile beyond Halberton. From Tiverton, take the B3391 and follow the signs to Halberton and Sampford Peverell, and you will come to the crossing about $2^1/2$ miles from the centre of the town.
- **PARKING:** There are two parking areas, one on either side of the canal. Try to park on the Halberton side, as that is where the path runs. But if that area is full, you can park on the other side and cross the bridge to start the walk.
- **LENGTH OF THE WALK:** 5 miles. Maps: OS Landranger 181 Minehead and Brendon Hills (start and finish), 192 Exeter and Sidmouth (middle section); OS Explorer 128 Taunton and Blackdown Hills (start and finish), 114 Exeter and the Exe Valley (middle section) (GR 998131).

THE WALK

1. From the parking area on the Halberton side of the canal, turn left and follow the towpath under the bridge. (If you have had to park on the other side of the canal, then cross the bridge and turn right.) It is delightfully tranquil along here and the canal, which has hardly any flow to it at all, is full of interest, with ducks, coots and moorhens on the water, and wild flowers along the banks in spring and summer.

After about 300 yards you come to another bridge. Follow the path up to a gate onto a road. Turn right to cross the bridge and then left on the other side to follow the opposite bank. You get an attractive view through the odd gaps in the hedge on your right as you go. About 700 yards further on you cross an aqueduct and about 400 yards beyond that you go under the East Manley Bridge (the names of the various bridges are indicated on plaques under the arches).

2. At the next bridge, which is the Manley Bridge, leave the towpath and go up to the lane above. Turn left across the bridge and follow the lane. After a while it begins to climb, but the hill is quite short. About 1/2 mile after leaving the canal the lane takes a sharp bend to the left; follow it round. There are extensive views to the left from up here, and you are quite likely to see pheasants in the fields and hedges around you.

3. When you come to a T-junction, turn left. It is a quiet, pretty, often flower-fringed lane, with more extensive views across the rolling farmland to the right. After a while it runs alongside the canal, although the bank and line of trees on your left hide the latter from view. It swings right, away from the canal and alongside a deep cutting – the track of the old railway, now dismantled.

4. At the next T-junction, turn left and follow the lane into Halberton. Keep to the main lane until you come to Church Path on your right, then turn right along it. Where the road ends, follow the surfaced path round to the right of the attractive church. At the path junction go left and then right along Pond Hill, past some pretty thatched cottages and the village pond, up to the main Tiverton to Sampford Peverell road. Turn right.

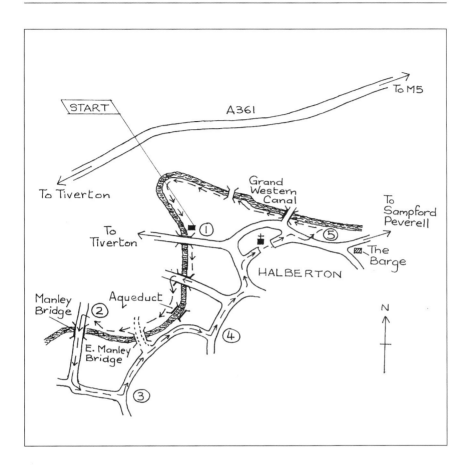

5. Follow the road for a short distance until you see a public footpath sign on your left, pointing up a track; turn up here. (If you want to visit the pub, then continue along the main road for about 300 yards and you will see it on your right.) Follow the track to a stile into a field. Go round to the right of the field and you will come to another stile. Do not cross it, but follow the fence round to the left until you come to yet another stile on your right. Cross this one and go across the next field to a fourth stile.

Turn sharp left beyond the stile, through a gate and back onto the canal towpath. After about 300 yards you go under a bridge and on the other side a very good view opens up on the left, across Halberton to the farms and hills beyond. This is another lovely

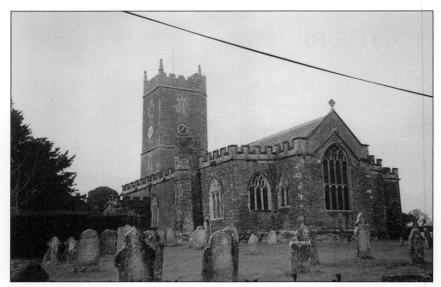

Halberton church.

stretch; the water hardly moves and the silence is only broken by the occasional 'plop' as a waterbird dives.

After another mile or so, the canal swings to the left, with a bank on your left which soon gives way to low hedges again, offering you further attractive views across the farms and woods to the hills beyond, with Halberton half left again. Continue for just over ¹/₂ mile and you will reach the parking area where you started.

PLACES OF INTEREST

The *Tiverton Museum* is one of the largest social history museums in the South-West, and illustrates the area's history going back to Roman times. Just north of Tiverton is *Knightshayes Court*, a Victorian house and garden owned by the National Trust. Still on a historical theme, *Bickleigh Castle*, 6 miles south of Tiverton, dates back 900 years. Also at Bickleigh is the *Yearlstone Vineyard*, where tours are available.

THE RIVER TAW AT NORTH TAWTON

Farm tracks, riverside paths, pretty woodland and hedgerows, beautiful views – this undemanding walk has them all. It follows a short stretch of the Tarka Trail, a lovely route that winds along the Taw and Torridge valleys, the setting for 'Tarka the Otter'.

The Barton, near North Tawton.

This walk follows a short stretch of the Tarka Trail, the beautiful route that stretches from Dartmoor to Barnstaple and takes in many of the scenes from Henry Williamson's classic *Tarka the Otter*, as it winds along beside the Taw. It starts at North Tawton, an interesting village a short distance from the river, which was once a centre of the wool trade, and which was granted a market as long ago as the 12th century. A sign of its former importance is the Broadhall or Town Hall in The Square, parts of which date back to the 15th century. Although it is now something of a backwater, it still boasts several shops, a hotel and an attractive pub, the Fountain Inn (telephone: 01837 82551). Situated in Exeter Street, just off High Street and a few yards off our route, this is full of atmosphere, and offers a wide variety of fare, ranging from sandwiches and ploughman's lunches to a mouthwatering array of main meals.

From North Tawton, we follow clear paths across farm fields to The Barton, a beautiful 16th-century manor house. Just beyond that we join the Tarka Trail for a pretty amble alongside the river before linking up with a quiet lane lined with often flowery hedgerows for a short distance. There then follows a lovely wooded stretch along the riverbank again, and we return to North Tawton along more farm paths and tracks and another quiet lane. To add to the other attractions of the route, there are some grand views to be enjoyed from time to time along the way.

- **HOW TO GET THERE:** North Tawton is just over $1/2$ mile north of the A3072 between Crediton and Okehampton, and is clearly signposted.
- **PARKING:** There is plenty of parking in the streets of North Tawton, especially along High Street and in The Square. Please park with consideration for others, however; some of the streets are narrow, and careless parking can block entrances or cause bottlenecks.
- **LENGTH OF THE WALK:** 4 miles. Maps: OS Landranger 191 Okehampton and North Dartmoor; OS Explorer 113 Okehampton (GR 663017).

THE WALK

1. Starting from The Square, walk south along High Street until you come to Barton Street on your right. Turn right here and follow Barton Street until it turns to the right and becomes Barton Hill. Go straight on here, following the public footpath sign, along a path beween hedges filled with seasonal wild flowers.

Cross a stile into a field, and keep to the left, alongside a bank. After a while the path bears right, diagonally across the field, to a gate. Go through and bear right to cross the next field. You come out by a warehouse; follow the broad track which runs to the left of it and you will come out onto a road. Turn right, and you will pass The Barton on your right.

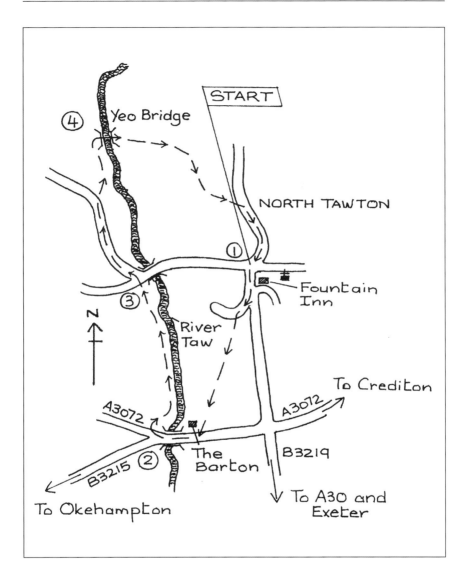

2. You cross two bridges; immediately beyond the second, turn right, following the Tarka Trail footpath sign. Go through a gate and follow the path to the right along the bank of the tree-fringed river. At the end of the field, follow the path round to the left. The water is almost motionless along here. The reason for this soon becomes

47

The River Taw, near North Tawton.

clear as you pass a weir, after which it flows much more rapidly as it cascades over the rocks below.

After a while you cross a wooden bridge and go through a rather dilapidated gate. Keep alongside the river as you cross the next field, and when it curves to the left, follow it round. When it curves to the right again, cut across the field to the road bridge you can see ahead of you.

3. Go through a turnstile and turn left along the road, then immediately right (signposted to Winkleigh). Follow this quiet, hedge-fringed lane for a little over 1/2 mile, past Week Barton and Bridge Farm, and when it bends sharply to the left, go right, following the Tarka Trail footpath sign. Cross the stile on your left, following the Tarka Trail waymark, rather than turning right to follow the other path. You are now back alongside the river; the path soon veers away from it for a short while, but then curves right to rejoin it.

Cross a stile into a delightful wood carpeted with flowers for much of the year, still with the river flowing placidly beside you on the right. Cross another stile to leave the wood and join a track.

4. Turn right to cross the river via Yeo Bridge. Follow the track as it goes to the right to a gate. Turn right again beyond the gate, onto another track. You pass the buildings of Yeo Farm on the left. Just before you come to a barn on your right and the track becomes a surfaced lane, turn left up another track, following the public footpath sign.

Go through a gate and round some farm cottages. Just past them you will find a small gate on the right, marked with a yellow waymark. Go through it and bear left to a stile, also with a waymark. Go straight across the next field. At the end are two gates; go through the right-hand one, which is waymarked.

Follow a rather overgrown track between hedges to a stile. On the other side, the path is a bit wet, but it soon becomes drier. The hedges along here are filled with flowers in season. You will come to a junction; turn right to a stile, and then immediately left on the other side. You get a lovely view ahead of you across the undulating farmland. Keep to the left, and after a few yards you will find a gate on your left; go through it and bear right across the next field to a stile in the far right-hand corner.

You are now faced with a choice of two paths, one going straight on and the other right; you need to go straight on. Cross another stile and cut diagonally across the field beyond, aiming for the far right-hand corner. Go through a gate and across a small yard to a stile, which leads onto a lane. Turn right and follow the lane for about 300 yards back to North Tawton.

PLACES OF INTEREST

At Winkleigh, about 6 miles away (north), is the *Square Gallery*, which has a display of work, mainly by West Country artists and craft workers. Okehampton (8 miles) is home to the *Museum of Dartmoor Life* and *Okehampton Castle*, a ruined Norman castle now in the hands of English Heritage.

WALK 8

THE EAST OKEMENT VALLEY

You get the opportunity to enjoy a variety of scenery on this walk as you follow quiet lanes and farm paths up to the edge of Dartmoor and then return to Okehampton through the beautiful woods that flank the East Okement River.

The leafy path by the East Okement River.

Okehampton is an interesting and attractive town at the confluence of the East and West Okement Rivers, on the northern edge of Dartmoor, and it is well worth exploring.

The walk starts by following the Tarka Trail, the long-distance route which takes in various sites associated with Henry Williamson's classic book *Tarka the Otter*. You stay on it through a delightful wood, up the valley of the East Okement River, and from there up to the edge of Dartmoor.

You return through another gorgeous wood on the opposite bank, passing the old Okehampton Station on your way back into

Okehampton. This has been refurbished and turned into a visitor centre and restaurant (there are also trains to Exeter on Sundays in the summer). You can stop here for refreshments if you are so minded. The old buffet has been very tastefully done up and now serves tea, coffee and a range of meals in a charming setting, inside or on the platform. There is no direct telephone line to the restaurant, but Hobby Horse Models, who run the complex (telephone: 01837 55330), can provide any information you may need. The complex is only open from Tuesday to Sunday in summer and Wednesday to Sunday in winter.

There are also plenty of alternative watering holes in Okehampton if the station restaurant is closed, including both pubs and tearooms. My recommendation would be the White Hart Hotel in Fore Street (telephone: 01837 54514), just 200 yards or so from the start of the walk, in the town centre.

- **HOW TO GET THERE:** Okehampton is just north of the A30 Exeter to Launceston road, and is reached via the B3260. It is clearly signposted from both directions.
- **PARKING:** The best place to park for this walk is the long-stay car park off Mill Road. If you are approaching from the Exeter direction, turn left off the main street before you cross the river, following the long-stay parking sign. If you are coming from the Launceston side, go through the centre of town and you will see it signposted to the right after the second bridge; do not follow the signs for Dartmoor parking which point right past the White Hart Hotel.
- **LENGTH OF THE WALK:** $4^1/_2$ miles. Maps: OS Landranger 191 Okehampton and North Dartmoor; OS Outdoor Leisure 28 Dartmoor; OS Explorer 113 Okehampton (GR 590951).

THE WALK

1. Leave the car park via some steps which lead up to a row of houses on the opposite side from the river. Go through an archway between two houses and turn right into Mill Road. When the road forks, go left, and at the traffic island at Simmons Way bear right; you will soon see a footpath sign pointing to Ball Hill, Father Ford and the East Okement valley.

Follow the road past Okehampton College, with a leat on your left. The road ends at a large car park. Go straight on through a gate

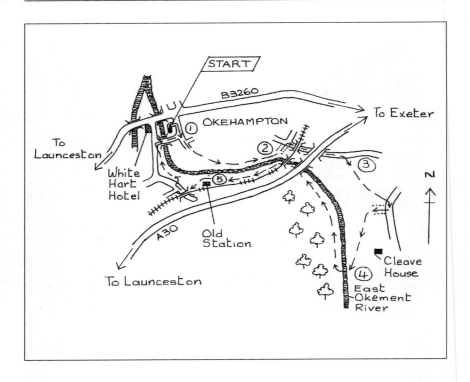

marked with the Tarka Trail waymark. This leads onto a track, with the leat now on the right. At the end of the track, go through a kissing gate and across the bottom of a field. Go through another kissing gate and across another field to a third kissing gate. Cross a track and go through another gate, also marked with the Tarka Trail waymark, into a wooded area.

You soon pass a field on your right, on the other side of which is the East Okement River. The path climbs slightly, and you can now see the river immediately below you. This is a most attractive area, with the woods stretching up the hill on the left and the river just visible – and audible – through the trees on the right. The path descends again and runs alongside the river for a short distance before bearing away from it again to a gate.

2. Go through the gate onto a track and turn left (signposted to the Exeter road). At the junction, turn right (signposted to a riding stable) and follow the lane under a railway line and then under the

Waterfall on the East Okement River.

A30. The lane winds to the left and the right, and you can see across to the moors on your right.

3. About 300 yards after passing under the A30, turn right through a gate, following the footpath sign which points to the road near Cleave House. Cross a small footbridge over a stream, and follow the path round to the left of a bank and into a field. Keep to the right, alongside a wall. At the top of the field, cross a stile and then cross a track and keep to the right of the next field to reach another stile. Go to the right of the row of trees on the other side, and when you get to the top of the field you will get a superb view to the right and back the way you have come.

Go through a gateway and bear left, following a path sign, to reach a stile leading onto a lane. Turn right and cross a cattle grid. After a few yards you will see a track on your right, signposted to West Cleave, the East Okement valley and the moor. Turn down it and at the end go through a gate onto open heathland. The track is very indistinct here, but bear left and it will soon become clearer. The views up here are magnificent: to Dartmoor on the left, across rolling farmland on the right, and over the wooded East Okement valley ahead.

Follow the track round the hill. It passes a wall on the left, and about 100 yards beyond that, it forks: the clearer route continues on round the hill, while a less distinct track branches off to the right. Take the latter and follow it as it slopes gently down through the gorse into the valley below, becoming more marked as it does so.

4. At the bottom, you will see a footbridge across the river. Cross over to a beautiful wood and turn right along the clear path alongside the river. This stretch of wood is carpeted with bluebells and wild garlic in the spring.

Where the path forks, take the right-hand route, which runs above the river. You pass an impressive waterfall and the path becomes rather rocky and wet as it descends to the riverbank, so take care. This is a lovely stretch, with the wooded hillside on the left and, if you are lucky, the sun dappling the river as it tumbles over a succession of rapids on the right. The path leaves the water briefly to cross a wall and then a footbridge. At the path junction on the other side, bear right to rejoin the river. At the next junction, go straight on (signposted to Okehampton). You pass under the A30

The old mill, Okehampton.

again and come to a gate. Beyond the gate, go straight on under the railway line (signposted to Station Road) to a gate leading onto a track.

This passes along the left of a field, slightly away from the river, and soon enters another lovely wood. From time to time you can just see the river below you through the trees. You pass a long clearing on your left and then the path re-enters the wood and you can see the sports fields of Okehampton College through the trees on the right.

5. Go through a gate onto a track. Just beyond a house on the right, you will see a sign pointing up to the left to the Station Visitor Centre. Go up some steps and you will come out at the station. If you do not want to stop for refreshments or to have a look round, go straight past the buildings into Station Road and turn right.

After a few yards, you will find a footpath sign on your right, pointing to Okehampton Park leisure grounds. Turn right and follow the path down to some steps. At the junction, go straight on to a surfaced road which runs alongside the river, through Simmons Park. Where the road forks, go right and through a white gate onto a road. Turn right and follow the road round to the left, passing the old mill on the right as you do so. After a few yards you will come to the row of houses you passed on the way out; go through one of the arches and down some steps to the car park.

PLACES OF INTEREST

The ruins of *Okehampton Castle*, on the outskirts of the town, are worth a visit. Now owned by English Heritage, it is Norman in origin and was once the home of the powerful Courtenay family. Nearby is the *Museum of Dartmoor Life*, with reconstructions and exhibits about the social history of the moor. And at Sticklepath, 4 miles away to the east, you will find the National Trust's *Finch Foundry*, a 19th-century water-powered forge, still in working order.

THE RIVER OTTER AT OTTERY ST MARY

Ottery St Mary is a bustling town, with much to interest the visitor, and it is an ideal starting point for this walk. The route follows the River Otter downstream through the fertile East Devon farmland to the village of Tipton St John. The return journey takes you up the opposite bank, through some pretty woodland and across farm fields, before veering away to return to Ottery along a quiet road.

The River Otter.

The Otter rises in the Blackdown Hills, just across the Devon/ Somerset border, and by the time it reaches Ottery St Mary it is a wide, tranquil waterway, flowing gently through farm fields.

Ottery is an attractive town, particularly noted for its beautiful old collegiate church. It is also famous as the birthplace of the poet Coleridge, whose father was rector here. It was a major centre of the wool industry, and towards the start of the walk you follow a leat, at the end of which is a unique 'tumbling weir' – a circular structure with the water cascading down into the middle – built to power a Georgian serge factory. Between the leat and the river is the Tumbling Weir Hotel and Restaurant (telephone: 01404 812752), which offers drinks and restaurant-type meals in a delightful location overlooking the water.

The walk follows the right bank of the Otter across farm fields to the thriving village of Tipton St John, passing another spectacular weir along the way. In the village you will find the Golden Lion Inn (telephone: 01404 812881), where a range of snacks and bar meals are available. The route then follows the opposite bank of the river, through a pretty wooded area, flower-filled for much of the year, and across more farm fields. The last $1/2$ mile or so is along a quiet road which takes you into the centre of Ottery.

It is an undemanding walk, but there is one particularly muddy stretch near Tipton St John, so appropriate footwear should be worn.

- **HOW TO GET THERE:** Ottery St Mary is just south of the A30 Exeter to Honiton road; it can be reached via the B3174 from the Exeter direction and via the B3177 from Honiton.
- **PARKING:** Use the Hind Street pay-and-display car park, which is signposted from both directions.
- **LENGTH OF THE WALK:** $5\,3/4$ miles. Maps: OS Landranger 192 Exeter and Sidmouth; OS Explorer 30 (to be renumbered 115) Exmouth and Sidmouth (GR 096955).

THE WALK

1. Turn right out of the car park, and follow Hind Street to a T-junction. Go straight on into a rather pleasant park. When you come to a raised flower bed in the middle of the path, turn left. Where the path goes to the right, follow it round to cross a small footbridge. Turn immediately left, past the Tumbling Weir Hotel.

The path runs alongside a pretty leat, which was constructed to supply water to an old corn mill, and later the serge factory. At the end you will see the tumbling weir. Follow the path round to the right and then left between the River Otter and the factory. It brings you out onto a main road. Turn right and cross St Saviour's Bridge.

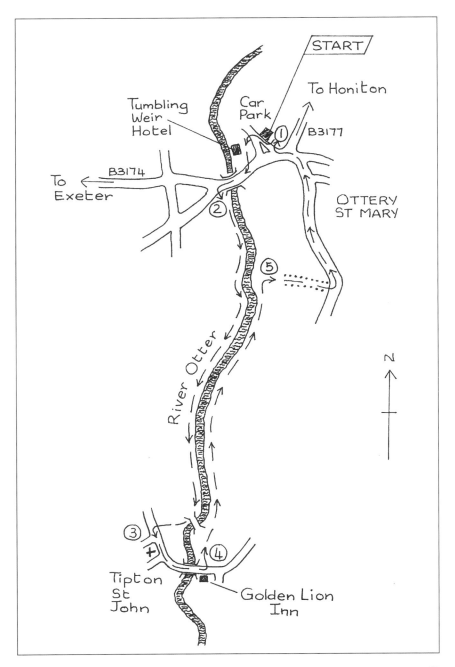

2. Immediately on the other side, turn left off the road, following the public footpath sign. You go down some steps and across a stile, and cross a small field to a narrow gateway alongside the river. Cross the next field to another stile, and at the end of the next field cross a footbridge, still keeping to the river, which flows swiftly but placidly through the farmland. You cross another footbridge, and at the end of the next field a stile and a footbridge. Here the river takes a wide sweep to the left; you should carry straight on to cut off the loop.

At the end of this field you meet up with the river again and cross a stile and another footbridge. At the other end of this field, you will see the raised embankment of a disused railway line on your right. Go over another stile and continue along the bank. You cross a muddy stretch followed by another two footbridges, and more fields, and soon you will see a rather spectacular weir on your left.

In the next field, the path follows the line of the river to the disused railway bridge you can see towards the right – it does not cut straight across to the bridge. When you reach the bridge, do not cross it, but follow the river round a bend. Go through a gate and turn right along a very muddy track away from the river. It is best to keep to the bank to the right of the track, or perhaps skirt round through the field even further to the right to avoid the worst of the mud. Go through a gate at the end onto a road.

3. Turn left and follow the road into Tipton St John. At the junction go straight on (signposted to Tipton St John and Newton Poppleford). You pass the church on your right. Carry straight on at the next junction (signposted to Tipton St John, Ottery St Mary and Sidmouth). The road curves round to the left and then crosses the river. You will see the Golden Lion Inn on your right. Follow the road for about 150 yards, passing the attractive, whitewashed Brook Cottage and Dolphin Cottage on your left.

4. Immediately beyond Dolphin Cottage, turn left up a narrow path, following the public footpath sign. The path leads you between a fence on the left and a bank on the right. You come to a stile, which leads you into a small stretch of woodland, alongside a stream. Cross another stile and continue through the trees, still with the stream on your left. You emerge onto some open ground, which leads into a field. Keep to the left, alongside the stream, to a stile on

The 'tumbling weir' near the start of the walk.

the left. Go down some steps and turn right to a gate leading into another field.

Keep to the left again to reach another gate, and then follow a short path to yet another gate which leads into the yard of Tipton Mill. Bear right up a track between the old buildings to a fourth gate and follow the track on the other side. Where the track turns right, go straight on, following the direction of a yellow waymark, to a stile leading into a field.

Keep to the left of this field and you can see the river down below you on the left. You soon see the weir again, and just beyond it the path leaves the field to go down to the riverbank. When you get there, you reach a stile and then, after a few yards, a second one. Keep to the left of the field beyond to a third stile.

Where the river takes a short loop to the left, leave the riverbank to climb some steps to a gate leading into a field. Keep to the left of the field and you will come to a stile on the left. Cross it, go down some steps and turn right to cross another stile into another field. Keep left again to reach another stile which takes you onto a track. Turn left, and just before you reach the gate at the end of the track turn right along a narrow path among some trees.

You cross another stile and then a stream, and follow the path to the left below a bank. At the end of the field climb the bank to a stile, followed by some steps and another stile. Turn left to keep to the left-hand side of the next field. You join a track; bear left and follow the track to a gate. On the other side, keep to the left of a field. After about 100 yards you will see a stile on your left; cross it and turn right to follow the path above the river. After a while you will come to some steps down a steep slope; go down and then bear right, and you will come to a stile which leads you to a track.

5. Turn right and go through a gate. Follow the track for about 500 yards to a gate into a road. Turn left. After just over ¹/₂ mile, this road takes you back to Ottery St Mary. Follow it into the centre of the town. At the first junction in the town centre, follow the main road round to the left, and at the second, follow it round to the left again. Immediately after this second junction, you will see Hind Street going off to the right; turn into it and the car park is on your right.

PLACES OF INTEREST

Just outside Ottery St Mary is *Cadhay House*, a 16th-century manor house which is open to the public. And a little further north (about 2 miles from Ottery) you will find *Escot Park and Gardens*, which has wild boar, otters, birds of prey and tropical fish in 20 acres of parkland. And if you are interested in lace, a visit to *Allhallows Museum* in Honiton (6 miles), with its displays of 500 years of lacemaking, is a must.

THE TEIGN GORGE

Follow the enchanting Teign valley upstream through a beautiful wooded gorge, then take a farm track and a pretty lane to visit the Iron Age hillfort of Cranbrook Castle, from where there are some stunning views. The return journey takes you back into woodland for the final descent back to the river. It is generally an easy walk, but there is a series of steady and quite long climbs to reach Cranbrook Castle.

Fingle Bridge.

Fingle Bridge, where this walk starts, is a 16th-century hump-backed bridge in a delightful spot in the depths of a National Trust wood. It is very popular, both for picnicking and for riverside walks, but this route follows some of the less frequented paths.

We accompany the River Teign upstream along one of its most beautiful stretches – a steep-sided, wooded gorge which was part of the estate of Castle Drogo, a superb early 20th-century country house designed by Sir Edwin Lutyens.

After following the river for about 1½ miles, we cut across, via a farm track, to a quiet lane flanked by banks and hedges to climb, steadily but in relatively easy stages, to Cranbrook Castle, where the remains of Iron Age fortifications can be seen. The views, both along the way and from Cranbrook Castle itself, are magnificent. The fortifications comprise a stone-faced rampart, with a ditch outside it, and a second rampart and ditch outside that. Interestingly, it was never completed – you will see that there are no fortifications on the northern side (the side facing the river). The reason for this will never be known, of course, but it could be that the hillfort was started in response to a particular threat which never materialised, and that the inhabitants then decided it was not worth the effort of continuing the rampart all the way round.

The Angler's Rest (telephone: 01647 281287), which is across the river from the start of the walk, is just the place to stop for refreshments, either before or after your walk. It offers a wide range of fare, from soups and simple bar snacks to steaks and fish dishes, as well as cream teas, coffees and so on. There is also a shop attached, which sells ice creams, locally made food products, gifts and books.

- **HOW TO GET THERE:** Turn south off the A30 Exeter to Okehampton road or east off the A382 between Moretonhampstead and Okehampton, following the signs to Drewsteignton. From Drewsteignton, follow the brown signs to Fingle Bridge.
- **PARKING:** The best place to park for this walk is in the car park across the bridge. The bridge is somewhat narrow, however, and if you are concerned about crossing it in a wide car, then you will find additional parking on the left-hand side of the road as you approach it. Be aware, however, that the area outside the Angler's Rest is for patrons of the pub only.
- **LENGTH OF THE WALK:** 4 miles. Maps: OS Landranger 191 Okehampton and North Dartmoor; OS Outdoor Leisure 28 Dartmoor (GR 743899).

THE WALK

1. The walk starts on the southern side of Fingle Bridge (the opposite side from the Angler's Rest). There is a gap in a fence on the upstream side; go through that and follow the path beyond

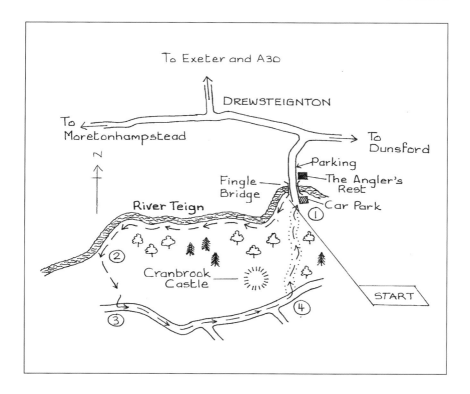

upriver. You soon cross a small footbridge; the area beyond it is carpeted with bluebells in the spring, with a mass of pink purslane along the bank. Soon you will find a footbridge on your left; you can either cross it to reach a track or continue alongside the river for a short distance until you come to some steps leading up to the track.

Either way, turn right along the track. This is a lovely stretch, with the river running swiftly on your right and the steep wooded slopes of the gorge on either side. You pass a weir, and beyond it the river flows more slowly and quietly. The track runs along the hillside, with the river now far below you, and the slope above carpeted with whortleberries.

When the track forks, go right to return to the riverbank again. Soon the dappled light of the broadleaved wood gives way to a darker, more closely packed conifer plantation, but after a while this merges into broadleaved woodland again. You will come to a large

65

Iron Age fortifications, Cranbrook Castle.

felled area, after which the track climbs slightly and you cross a small rivulet by an old wall as you re-enter the wood.

A few hundred yards later, the track climbs away from the river and a broad path leads off to the right towards a deserted building. Follow that, keeping to the left of the building, and you will soon join up with the track again by a gate. Bear right past the gate, still following the path. Where it forks, you can go either way. The left-hand path runs along the top of a large pipeline, which calls for a reasonably good sense of balance, while the right-hand one goes alongside the water, but is somewhat more rocky. Beyond the pipeline they join up again.

You will soon come to another weir, with a sluice alongside. The path climbs up to the left of the sluice and continues alongside a wall.

2. When you see a metal footbridge across the river, look out for a stone stile across the wall on your left. Cross it onto a track and turn right to follow the track across Whiddon Park. Ignore the diversion going right across a bridge and follow the main track for about 500 yards until it curves to the right to a gate leading onto a lane.

3. Turn left and follow the lane between banks and hedges, flower-filled in season, as it climbs steadily. It soon levels off and you get a grand view over to your right. After a short level stretch it begins to climb again. It is beautifully still along here, with only the bleating of the sheep and the occasional birdsong to break the silence. The hill is a long one, but the views across the farmland to the moors in the distance make it worth while.

At the junction, go straight on (signposted to Clifford Bridge and Dunsford). Just beyond it the lane levels off again before starting the final ascent. At the top you come to another junction; go straight on again (again signposted to Clifford Bridge and Dunsford).

4. About 300 yards beyond this junction is a track going off to the left; turn onto it and after a few yards you will see a public footpath sign pointing to Fingle Bridge and Cranbrook Castle. After about 100 yards, go through a gate on the left, following the signpost to Cranbrook Castle. Climb the short hill beyond to the fortifications. It is easy to understand why our Iron Age forebears chose this site for their hillfort – it is a commanding situation, with stunning views all around.

When you have explored the fortifications, retrace your steps down the hill and through the gate, and turn left down the track. It is a lovely, tree-lined route which takes you down to the wood above the river. Just inside the wood there is a junction; follow the main track round to the left (signposted to Fingle Bridge). It twists and turns as it descends steeply through the wood, emerging just by the bridge.

PLACES OF INTEREST

Castle Drogo is only 1 mile beyond Drewsteignton, on the road to Moretonhampstead. Now owned by the National Trust, it is a fine example of an early 20th-century country house, with outstanding views. About 7 miles beyond that, on the other side of Moretonhampstead, is the *Miniature Pony Centre*, which has a variety of other animals besides ponies for children to handle and cuddle.

THE RIVER EXE AND THE EXETER CANAL

Despite its urban and semi-urban setting, this is a beautiful and tranquil walk. It is also full of historical interest as it follows the River Exe from Exeter Quay down to the area known as Countess Wear and returns along the Exeter Canal. It is very easy going, mainly along surfaced paths and lanes.

A refreshment stop on the walk.

The history of the River Exe and the Exeter Canal between Exeter itself and Countess Wear is in essence a story of centuries of conflict between the city and the Courtenay family, who held the Earldom of Devon and owned most of the land to the south, including the important Manor of Topsham.

The story begins in the 13th century when Isabella de Fortibus, Countess of Devon, built two weirs across the river and leats to supply water to the mills and industries she was establishing in the area, which hence became known as Countess Wear. Although these weirs affected Exeter's salmon fisheries, a wide enough gap was left between them for ships to be able to continue upriver to the city's quay.

However, Isabella's successor, Hugh de Courtenay, saw in the weirs an opportunity to increase his revenues at Exeter's expense. In the 14th century he narrowed the gap so that it became impossible for ships to pass and they were forced to discharge their cargoes (and pay the duties on them) at his own quay at Topsham. With this single act he brought to an end a maritime tradition which stretched back to pre-Roman times.

The enraged citizens of Exeter petitioned a succession of kings on a number of occasions, but to no avail – the Courtenays were too powerful a force in the land, and the weirs remained. After two centuries of conflict, however, they were at last able to restore the city to its position as a major port. In 1538 the head of the Courtenay family, Henry, Marquis of Exeter, was accused of treason by Henry VIII. He was executed and all his lands were confiscated. This gave the city fathers their chance to reopen the maritime trade. They tried to demolish the hated weirs but failed, so instead they built a canal to bypass them. It originally ended just below Countess Wear, but in the 17th century it was extended further downsteam, and at the same time the quay was also extended to its present length.

Our walk starts at the head of the canal, in the heart of the historic quay area, much of which has been beautifully restored – and where restoration has not been possible, tastefully rebuilt. You then follow the Exe downstream to one of Isabella's weirs and the leat that it supplies before turning back to return via the canal to the harbour. Although you will pass some suburban housing along the way, for most of its length the route manages to avoid the sights and sounds of the city, and the birdlife on the river – even as high as the Canal Basin – is a constant source of interest.

There are two pubs I would recommend if you are looking for refreshment along the way. The first is the Port Royal (telephone: 01392 272360), which is near the beginning of the walk, overlooking the river. It has a wide-ranging menu, including the usual bar snacks and main meals such as steak, curry and chilli. If you would like a break during the walk, a detour of 100 yards or so will take you to the Double Locks Hotel (telephone: 01392 256947), about three-quarters of the way round. Here you can enjoy anything from sandwiches and jacket potatoes to lasagne or ham and egg on the terrace right on the bank of the canal.

- **HOW TO GET THERE:** The walk starts at the Piazza Terracina, a large open space at the head of the Canal Basin in Haven Road, Exeter. To reach it, follow the brown signs to Exeter Quay; Haven Road is off Alphington Street. Alternatively, you can walk down from the city centre and join the walk at The Quay.
- **PARKING:** The most convenient car park for the Canal Basin is Haven Banks, which is signposted off to the right just beyond it.
- **LENGTH OF THE WALK:** 5 miles. Maps: OS Landranger 192 Exeter and Sidmouth; OS Explorer 114 Exeter and the Exe Valley (GR 922918). A street map of Exeter might also be useful, particularly for finding your way to the start.

THE WALK

1. If you have parked at the Haven Banks car park, follow the path at the far end from the vehicle entrance, which is signposted to the Maritime Museum (which is now closed). This will bring you out at the Piazza Terracina. Cross it and turn left to go round the shops and flats, alongside the river. There is a suspension footbridge across the river just behind them; cross it and turn immediately right to go over another footbridge. You can make a short detour to the left here if you wish, and visit the handsome 17th-century Custom House. Otherwise follow the river round to join The Quay. Along here you will pass several storage vaults built into the cliff, which are now used mainly as craft shops, as well as the Quay House interpretation centre.

Keep to the riverside, first along The Quay and then along a footpath. You will usually find large numbers of birds on the river – mainly gulls but also cormorants and ducks. Soon you will come to a suspension bridge on your right. Here the main route crosses over the path leading from the bridge and goes straight on into Belle Isle Park and out the other side. Dogs are not allowed in the park, however, so if you have one with you, you will have to turn left, and then right at the T-junction. At the path crossing, go straight on and soon the path through the park joins the route you are on from the right.

On the other side of the park the path continues to follow the line

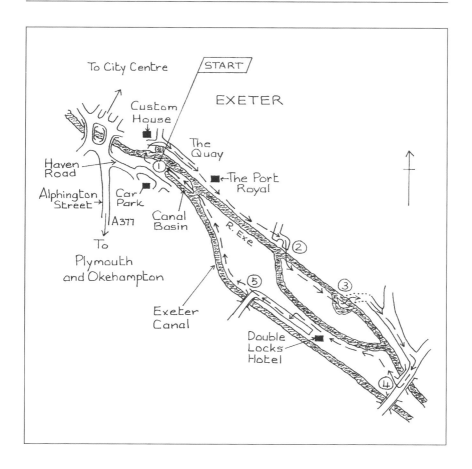

of the river, and eventually comes out onto a road; go straight across down a lane (signposted to the river and playing fields).

2. Follow the lane round to the right past a children's play area and cross a bridge just below a weir – this is one of Countess Isabella's weirs. On the other side turn left (signposted to Countess Wear). This path takes you alongside a wide, fast-flowing leat on your left, with playing fields on the right and the main channel of the river beyond them.

Where the leat divides, cross a footbridge and follow the path through some trees between the two channels. It goes to the left, through a kissing gate and past a house. At the T-junction go left to

Countess Wear House, Exeter.

cross the other channel and follow a track to the right. As you go you pass the remains of the Countess Wear Paper Mill on your right. The mill operated from the 17th century until 1885.

3. The track becomes a lane and goes to the left, where it joins a road; turn right. The road becomes a narrow lane and then an unsurfaced track before joining another road; turn right again. This road takes you above the river, past a youth hostel and the very attractive Countess Wear House, and emerges at a T-junction; turn right and cross the river via the busy road bridge.

4. Immediately on the other side turn right off the road down a track. At the end go left through a kissing gate and follow the track round and through a gateway, with the river on your right. It takes you through a kissing gate; immediately on the other side, turn left to cross a stile and go up some steps to a road. Turn left if you want to call in at the Double Locks Hotel, right to continue the walk. Follow the road, which is little used as it leads only to the Double Locks, for about a mile until it takes a sharp turn to the left to cross the canal.

5. Go straight on, through a parking area, to join a path, still alongside the canal, with some playing fields on your right.

As you approach the city centre, you will find a somewhat unsightly trading estate on the other side of the canal, but it is partially screened by trees and soon gives way to some very attractive waterside housing. The path is now tarred and soon turns to the left across a lock. On the other side turn right (signposted to the Canal Basin and ferry) and follow the path and road back to the Piazza Terracina.

PLACES OF INTEREST
In addition to the *Custom House*, which you pass along the route, Exeter has many other attractions, including several museums, the magnificent *cathedral*, the ancient *city walls* and *underground passages*. About 8 miles north-east of the city is *Killerton House*, an 18th-century National Trust property with lovely gardens.

BRANSCOMBE AND THE SOUTH DEVON COAST PATH

A pleasant amble down the valley to the sea is followed by a fairly stiff but short climb to the coast path, where you are rewarded with an excellent view. A delightful wooded stretch comes next, and then more open country, with a spectacular view along the coast. The return journey is along a quiet lane with pretty hedgerows and you finish with a stroll through the charming village of thatched and slate-roofed cottages.

The beach at Branscombe.

The village of Branscombe is in fact made up of five hamlets, descriptively if unimaginatively called Street, Church, Bridge, Vicarage and Great Seaside, separated by short stretches of open country. The two largest are Street on the western side and Vicarage to the east, with Church and Bridge between the two and Great Seaside on the coast. It is a delightful village, comprising a mixture of stone and whitewashed cottages, some thatched and some roofed with slate. The church is particularly interesting, incorporating as it does a variety of styles: Saxon, Norman, Elizabethan and 18th-century.

Surprisingly, it is not located in either of the two main centres, but tucked away in between, surrounded by its own hamlet. The reason for this is said to be so that it could not be seen by the Viking raiders who plundered this stretch of the coast. The ploy seems to have worked, as it did indeed escape pillaging.

Towards the end of this walk you have the chance to explore a large part of the village, but it begins with a pleasant stroll through fields, past the old village bakery (now a National Trust tearoom) to Manor Mill, which is also owned by the National Trust. The mill is open on Sunday afternoons from April to November, and also on Wednesday afternoons from July to September.

From the mill you continue down the valley to the sea, where you join the South Devon Coast Path. Most of the first section of this path in fact runs a short distance away from the coast, through a beautiful deciduous wood, but it soon comes out onto the cliff top again, and you get some quite stunning views along the coast. The return leg is along a pretty, often flower-filled lane and then you have a delightful stroll through three of the hamlets that make up the village, finishing at the old forge, now also owned by the National Trust but still functioning, with two resident blacksmiths.

The village boasts two pubs. In the Street area, and on the route of this walk, is the Fountain Head (telephone: 01297 680359), a homely, atmospheric establishment which stocks the local Branscombe beer and serves a selection of bar meals. At the other end, in the Vicarage area, is the Mason's Arms (telephone: 01297 690300), a creeper-clad inn which involves a slight detour and has less of a 'local' feel, but which serves excellent food, ranging from sandwiches and snacks to main meals.

- **HOW TO GET THERE:** Branscombe is about $2^1/_2$ miles south of the A3052 between Sidmouth and Seaton.
- **PARKING:** There are two car parks in the village, one in the Bridge area and the other at Great Seaside. The route description starts at the former, but if that is full you can use the latter, joining the walk where it reaches the coast (point 2) and finishing with the stroll across the fields described at the beginning of the route. Both car parks are signposted from the road through Branscombe.

- **LENGTH OF THE WALK:** 5 miles. Maps: OS Landranger 192 Exeter and Sidmouth; OS Explorer 30 (to be renumbered 115) Exmouth and Sidmouth (GR 197887).

THE WALK

1. Turn right out of the Bridge car park and then almost immediately left through a gate marked 'Path to Bakery and Mill'. This takes you past the Old Bakery to a footbridge and then to a gate. Cross the field on the other side to another gate, then cross another footbridge to yet another gate. Bear left alongside a leat to a fourth gate. Cross a track and go through a fifth gate to Manor Mill.

Go round to the left of the mill, down some steps and along a track to a gate. Turn right and go through a small gate immediately on the right. Follow the path along the left-hand side of a field. At the end, go straight on through a gate, signposted to Branscombe Mouth. (If you want to go to the Mason's Arms, however, turn left just before the gate, following the sign to the village.)

Keep to the left of the next field, with a stream on the other side of it. At the end go through a gate and turn right (signposted to Branscombe Mouth) and cross a small footbridge. Go through another gate and follow the path round to the left to reach the beach. If you are starting from the Great Seaside car park, this is where you join the walk – cross the stream to meet the path.

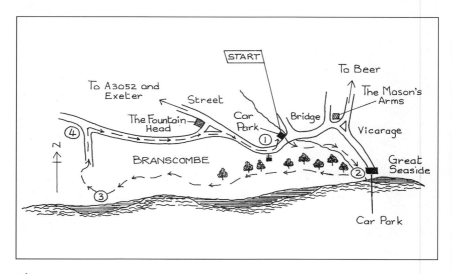

Manor Mill, Branscombe.

2. Turn sharp right through a kissing gate (signposted 'Coast Path to Weston Mouth') and cross a field to a gate. Go through and bear left to climb up another field. You get a lovely view to the right across the village and, if you look back, another along the beach to Beer Head. Go through a kissing gate and up some steps which wind to the right and to the left. The climb is pretty steep, but the view along the beach from the top is superb.

Near the top, you enter a pretty wooded area, with a wealth of wild flowers all around for much of the year. You cross a stile and continue through the trees, then along the top of a field and into the trees again. You cross another stile and the path broadens into a track. At the next path junction, turn left, following the Coast Path sign to Weston Mouth, and at the end bear right, still following the Coast Path sign, and then right again, as indicated by the yellow waymark. At the top go half left and cross the open space to a stile. You now get a spectacular view along the coast ahead of you, and another good view back the way you have come.

Cross another stile into a field and keep left. Just beyond a gate on the right you will come to a stile; cross it and bear left. The path curves right up a valley and then goes left to cross a stile. It goes down into a dip and then up the other side to another stile. Beyond it, the view ahead opens up again from time to time through the bushes on the left.

3. Cross another stile, and immediately beyond it turn right across yet another one. Keep to the right of the meadow to reach a gate, and keep to the right of the next field. Curve left round a house and cross a stile to a track; follow it round to the right to join a surfaced lane, with a bank on the right filled with flowers in season.

4. At the T-junction, turn right along another lane fringed by often flower-filled hedges. As you follow it, the view east along the coast opens up again. After about a mile, it brings you back to Branscombe. As you enter the village, turn left to reach the Fountain Head or go straight on to bypass it. Follow the lane past the charming scattering of cottages and the church back to the car park.

The Old Bakery.

PLACES OF INTEREST

Branscombe's *Manor Mill*, which you pass on the walk, is worth a visit. There is also a number of attractions in the nearby towns and villages. A few miles to the east, near Beer, you will find the *Beer Quarry Caves*, a network of caverns and quarries stretching back to Roman times. Also at Beer is *Pecorama*, which offers rides on miniature trains, as well as exhibitions of model railways. About $1^1/_2$ miles beyond Beer is Seaton, from where the *Seaton Tramway* operates, with tram rides up the Axe valley to Colyton. Four miles in the opposite direction, on the way to Sidmouth, you can visit the *Donkey Sanctuary*, and 6 miles to the north of Branscombe is *Farway Countryside Park*, which offers nature trails, as well as farm animals which children can feed and handle.

DAWLISH WARREN:
BEACH AND ESTUARY

This route does a circuit of the beautiful and internationally famous nature reserve of Dawlish Warren, with its wealth of wild flowers and birds. It is a delightful walk at any time but it is of particular interest in autumn and winter, when enormous flocks of waders can be seen on the beaches and mudflats.

The pond at Dawlish Warren.

Dawlish Warren Nature Reserve is centred around a 1^1/$_2$-mile double sandspit jutting out into the estuary of the Exe. It comprises a number of different habitats, including mudflats, dunes and reed beds, in addition to the beautiful, long beach which makes the area so popular with holidaymakers, and its importance to wetland birds is internationally recognised.

About 180 types of bird are recorded here each year, and in winter it is not unusual for as many as 20,000, comprising perhaps

30 or so species, to be seen at any one time. Among the waders to be found here are black-tailed godwits, greenshanks, curlews and sandpipers, and there are also many other species, including chiffchaffs, Brent geese, dunnets and peregrine falcons. But the Warren is not only a Mecca for birdwatchers. It is home to a wide variety of plants and wild flowers, and some of the views along the coast and up the River Exe are outstanding, so that everyone should find something here to enjoy, whatever their interest.

The walk starts in the main car park at the western end of the nature reserve, alongside the holiday shops and amusement arcades which are testimony to the area's popularity as a holiday resort. You soon turn your back on these, however, and follow the beach to the Exe estuary. After rounding Warren Point at the end of the spit, you skirt some mudflats before turning inland into the central area. There is also the chance to visit a bird hide overlooking the mudflats and salt marshes.

The central area has altered over the last 50 years from a tidal inlet to salt marsh, to freshwater marsh and finally to grassland, and its vegetation reflects all these different habitats. Your route takes you past a large pond and reed beds to an interesting visitor centre.

Alongside the car park there is a kiosk selling soft drinks, ice creams and snacks, but it is only open during the summer. For more substantial fare all year round, try the Mount Pleasant Inn (telephone: 01626 863151), about 300 yards from the car park, on the Dawlish road. This is a large, family-friendly pub with a menu to satisfy all needs, from light snacks to filling three-course meals.

- **HOW TO GET THERE:** Dawlish Warren is the name both of the nature reserve and of the village which has sprung up alongside it. It lies to the east of the A379 between Dawlish and Exeter, and can be reached from the south by turning right just beyond Dawlish, and from the north by turning left just beyond Starcross.
- **PARKING:** There is a large car park near the beach. Turn off the road that runs through the village (left if you are coming from Starcross, right if you are coming from Dawlish), following the signs to Dawlish Warren Station and Warren Golf Club. Go under the railway line and the car park is on your left.
- **LENGTH OF THE WALK:** 2$^{1}/_{2}$ miles. Maps: OS Landranger 192 Exeter and Sidmouth; OS Explorer 31 (to be renumbered 110) Torquay and Dawlish (GR 979786).

THE WALK

1. You will find a boardwalk leading from the car park through a picnic area towards the beach. When you get there, turn left, either along the beach itself or along a surfaced path which runs above it. As you go you get a very good view across the Exe estuary. If you are following the path, you will come to a barrier at the end, beyond which is a sandy path along the dune.

By now you will have left the holiday area behind you, and it is delightful to wander along the quiet beach, with the attractive view of Exmouth across the estuary ahead of you and the dunes, with their mantle of marram grass and wild flowers, alongside. But do

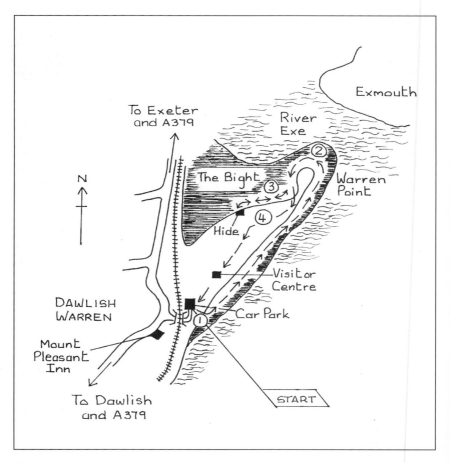

The Bight.

take heed of the notices along the way which explain how you can avoid disturbing the flocks of birds which use the estuary. If the tide is high, for example (with the water up to the red-topped groyne posts), you are asked to keep off the beach altogether and use the dune path.

2. When you reach the estuary, follow the beach round to the left around Warren Point. As you go round the corner, you get a very good view up the river to the hills around Exeter. Keep following the beach round to enter the inlet known as the Bight. Soon you will be forced to turn inland slightly to avoid some mudflats. Curve round to the right, between the dunes on your left and the mudflats on your right.

3. About halfway round you will find a path leading left, up into the dunes. If you want to visit the bird hide you can see round to the right, go straight on round the mudflats. (When you have finished there, you will have to retrace your route back to the path junction.) The path leads you through the dunes to avoid a golf course, and runs alongside the beach on the other side.

4. Near the end of the golf course there is a fork, with one path following the beach and the other going right, back among the dunes. Take the latter route, which follows the edge of the golf course for a short distance. You then pass a reed bed, and just beyond it there is another fork. Go left to join a major track, and bear right to follow it through the middle of the dunes.

You pass a pond on your right and then the visitor centre. This is worth a brief stop, as there are displays and information about the reserve. You then continue along the track to a gate; bear right beyond it to return to the car park.

PLACES OF INTEREST

Starcross, 2½ miles north of Dawlish Warren, is home to the *Brunel Atmospheric Railway*, a historic building which incorporates I. K. Brunel's atmospheric railway and other scientific exhibits. Another 2 miles beyond that is *Powderham Castle*, the 15th-century home of the Earls of Devon. In the other direction, at Shaldon (6 miles) you will find the *Shaldon Wildlife Trust*, a small zoo which specialises in rare and endangered species.

DARTMOOR AND THE EAST DART RIVER

*This walk combines a riverside ramble with some stunning moorland scenery. It gives you the opportunity to experience the awesome splendour of Dartmoor without too much effort. It must be remembered, however, that this **is** a moorland walk, and you cannot expect to find all the 'mod cons' provided on other routes – there are not always clear paths to follow, for example, and rivers and streams are crossed by stepping stones or rocks rather than footbridges. But provided you accept this and go suitably shod, you are in for a treat.*

The clapper bridge, Postbridge.

Dartmoor has been described as the last wilderness in southern England, and this circular route gives you a taste of its wildness and grandeur – from the highest point on the walk you can see the barren moor stretching away for miles in every direction, with not a house, not a road and hardly a tree in sight. And whereas the courses of other rivers are marked by wooded valleys or tree-lined floodplains, the banks of the peaty East Dart are at times hardly distinguishable from the surrounding moorland.

There is also a great deal of historical interest along the route. You pass through some old tin workings, dating back to the Middle Ages or earlier, when tin was panned from the streams and rivers of the area. You will also see reminders of more recent peat extraction on the higher ground, and in Postbridge, alongside the present road bridge, is an old clapper bridge which is probably about 500 years old.

The twin stone circles of Grey Wethers, on the slopes of Sittaford Tor, provide further interest. Dating back to the Bronze Age (although subsequently restored), they obviously had some ritual significance, but what that might have been is not certain. There is also a legend associated with them. It is said that at one time the men of the nearby town of Chagford had a novel way of punishing errant wives. They were chased up onto the moor, and after being put through a variety of other trials were brought to Grey Wethers. Here each woman had to kneel in front of a stone and pray for forgiveness. If she was forgiven, nothing happened and she could go home. If, however, her sins were too awful, then the stone would topple over and crush her!

Refreshments can be had at the East Dart Hotel in Postbridge (telephone: 01822 880213), which offers a range of home-made bar food, from pasties and rolls to more substantial main meals, as well as a restaurant menu.

- **HOW TO GET THERE:** Postbridge, where the walk starts, is on the B3212 between Princetown and Moretonhampstead.
- **PARKING:** In the National Park car park in the village. There is no parking fee as such, but a donation is requested.
- **LENGTH OF THE WALK:** 7½ miles. Maps: OS Landranger 191 Okehampton and North Dartmoor; OS Outdoor Leisure 28 Dartmoor (GR 647788).

THE WALK
1. Leave the car park via the gap in the bank just to the left of the Information Centre, and turn right up a track. Ignore the public bridleway sign pointing off to the left after a few yards and carry

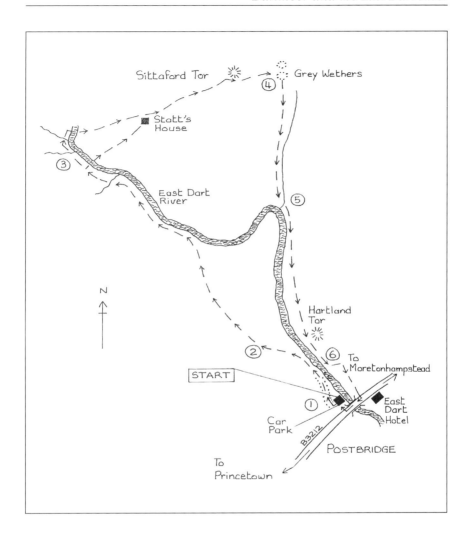

straight on, with a wall on your left. You cross four small stone footbridges, and the track narrows to a path. You will soon see the East Dart River tumbling over the rocks to your right, and you come to a gate.

2. Follow the clear path on the other side as it runs along the side of a hill, climbing away from the river. When you come to another gate in a wall ahead of you, bear left along the wall. The path veers slightly away from the wall, but remains fairly clear. You can now see the moors stretching away in all directions, with the river twisting away to the right.

The path joins a track, which soon crosses a stream via a ford; there are stepping stones a little to the left. You come to another stream; if it is in spate, you may have to go a few yards upstream to find a place to cross. The path climbs gently but steadily uphill, becoming less distinct as it does so. Keep more or less to the fence on your left as you climb. When you get to the top of the hill, go through a gate in the wall ahead.

Bear right along a track, which peters out after a few yards. Keep straight on, aiming in the general direction of the large rock on the horizon. There is a path which skirts to the left of it, but it is not very clear, and in any case it does not matter if you stray off it, because as long as you keep to the right general direction, you will see the river below you as you come over the brow of the hill.

Make your way down to the river and turn left to follow it upstream. You will pass a rather spectacular waterfall, and a little later the river turns to the right at the steep-sided gorge called Sandy Hole Pass. You can either keep to the bank and follow it through the pass or take the path which climbs up above it. If there has been a lot of rain I would recommend the latter route, as the riverside path can become boggy.

If you follow the riverbank, you will find that the path bears left when you emerge from Sandy Hole Pass to avoid a large marshy area, and joins up with the higher route. You cross a stream; once across it, go straight on to rejoin the river, passing through some old tin workings as you go.

3. Continue to follow the river until you come to a place where you can cross. There are some rocks about 400 or 500 yards from the stream, and if the water is not too high you should be able to cross there. If the water is high, however, you may need to continue upriver for some distance until you reach a suitable crossing point.

Once across the river, climb the hill ahead. Depending on where you have crossed, you may have to traverse a slight dip before the final ascent. At the top you will find an old ruined peat-cutters' hut called Statt's House – either straight ahead of you or slightly to the right. The views from up here are stunning – a $360°$ panorama. Ahead of you, you will see the large, flat-topped outcrop of Sittaford

The East Dart River out on the moor.

Tor, with a clear path running up to it from Statt's House. Follow that path, crossing a slightly boggy valley as you go.

When you reach Sittaford Tor, go through the ruined wall on your right and then cross the next wall via a ladder stile just to the right of the tor. Carry straight on, parallel to the wall on your left, and as you go down towards the valley ahead you will see the Grey Wethers circles; make your way down to them.

4. Turn right at Grey Wethers and take the broad, grassy path down towards a stream and then, as it narrows, along the side of the valley. Follow the path for about a mile, crossing a small stream along the way, and you will see the East Dart coming down from the right.

5. Go down to the stream on your left and find a place to cross it where it joins the river. Follow the path on the other side, along the bank of the river. You come to a gate; go through and continue to follow the path on the other side, with the river cascading down on your right. There are blue-waymarked posts from time to time to guide you, but the path is reasonably clear.

Go through a gap in a wall and bear left, following the direction of the waymark. As you follow the path, now some distance from the river, you will still find the odd waymarked post to ensure that you do not go wrong. The path runs just below Hartland Tor and then goes down towards the river again. It brings you to a gate; go through it and along a short paved path to another gate. Follow the path on the other side to a gap in the old wall on your right; go through and turn left to reach another gate.

6. Turn left immediately after this gate, to skirt along the edge of a field. At the end turn right, still keeping to the edge of the field, and you will come to a gate; go through and along the track on the other side to another gate, leading onto a road. The East Dart Hotel is along the road to your left. To return to the car park, turn right and cross the river. As you do so, you will see the old clapper bridge on your left.

PLACES OF INTEREST

To the north-east, 6 miles along the Moretonhampstead road, there is the *Miniature Pony Centre* which, in addition to the ponies which give it its name, has a variety of other farm animals for children to handle. And at Princetown, 4 miles in the other direction, you will find the *High Moorland Visitor Centre*, which has displays and exhibitions about the history, geology and wildlife of Dartmoor.

BECKY FALLS AND THE RIVER BOVEY

*This is a superb amble which takes in two gorgeous wooded valleys –
those of the Becka Brook and the River Bovey – visiting the lovely
Becky Falls along the way. The route is almost all woodland and,
apart from one long but steady hill near the beginning, it is fairly
easy going. Some sections can become rather wet, however, so
sensible footwear is recommended.*

The Becka Brook.

Becky Falls is a delightful spot which is very popular with visitors. It
is a private estate comprising 50 acres of woodland, and has a
tearoom and gift shop. The falls themselves are officially called
Becka Falls, and that is what appears on the maps, but the place is
universally known locally by its corrupted name. Also, it would be
better described as a cascade than as falls, since although the drop is

70 feet, the water tumbles over the boulders in stages rather than in a single rush.

Unfortunately the falls themselves can only be visited when the tearoom complex is open (10 am to 6 pm from Easter to November), but there are plenty of other opportunities to enjoy the beauty of this stretch of water. You then cut across to the equally lovely Bovey valley and meander along the wooded riverbank for over a mile.

There are two places where you can stop for refreshments along the way. The tearoom at Becky Falls is about a third of the way round the route, and serves light meals and cream teas when it is open. For more substantial fare throughout the year, call in at the Kestor Inn at Manaton (telephone: 01647 221204), a friendly pub which offers a wide range of fare, from bar food through light snacks to full restaurant meals.

- **HOW TO GET THERE:** Turn west off the A382 at Bovey Tracey and follow the signs towards Manaton. You will pass the entrance to Yarner Wood on your left and shortly afterwards the road takes a fairly sharp turn to the left, along the top of Trendlebere Down. Just after the bend you will see a parking area on the right; that is where the walk starts.
- **PARKING:** In the parking area.
- **LENGTH OF THE WALK:** 5½ miles. Maps: OS Landranger 191 Okehampton and North Dartmoor; OS Outdoor Leisure 28 Dartmoor (GR 783793).

THE WALK

1. Take the path that runs down the hill from the parking area, away from the road. It soon joins a track; turn left and follow it down alongside a wood. You can hear the River Bovey through the trees on your right.

Once you reach the valley, you will cross a small stream coming in on your left. Continue along the track, with the wood on your right and the steep slope of Trendlebere Down on your left. Soon that slope also becomes wooded and you will come to a junction. Keep straight on (signposted to Manaton). The water you can hear on your right now is not the Bovey but its tributary the Becka Brook, which will be keeping you company for the first part of the walk.

In fact, you soon meet up with the brook, with a footpath running

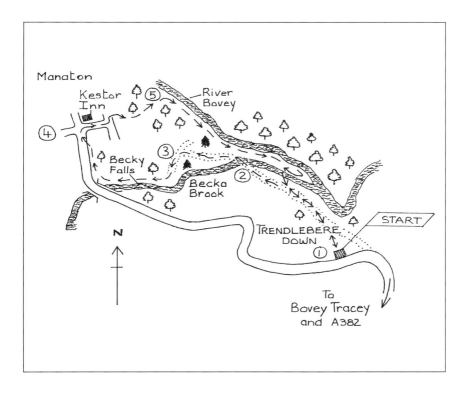

across a bridge to the right. Go straight on along the track (signposted to Manaton again). You cross another rivulet coming down from the left. The track and the brook diverge from time to time and then come together again.

2. The track finally turns right to cross the brook, goes through a gate and then curves to the left. The light and airy woodland through which you have been walking now gives way to a dark and densely planted conifer plantation. Keep following the track through as it starts to climb up the side of the valley, away from the brook. When you come to a fork, take the right-hand route, following the path sign. This takes you sharply round to the right and then to the left, climbing steadily as it does so. It levels off for a while and then there is one final climb to a junction.

3. Turn left (signposted to Becka Falls and the B3344). You will be

A row of thatched cottages at Water.

pleased to know that from now on it is downhill almost all the way. The track runs along the top edge of the plantation, with a bank on the right. You can still hear the Becka Brook down on your left as the track narrows to a path and you cross a stile into a broadleaved wood. After a little while you will see a path leading down some steps on the left. You can go down here for a lovely view of the brook cascading over the boulders. The main route down to the falls is a little further on, and there is a viewing platform from which you get a superb view, but it is only open at the same times as the tearoom (Easter to November). Whichever path you take, I strongly recommend that you visit the falls.

After visiting them, climb back up to the main path and turn left to continue the walk. After a while you will find a footbridge over the brook on your left. On the other side is the tearoom and gift shop. If you do not want to visit them, go straight on, following the yellow public footpath waymarks rather than the blue or red ones, which are nature trails around the Becky Falls estate.

The path leaves the brook, veering off to the right into the wood. You soon meet up with a small tributary of the Becka Brook, and then leave it again as you cross a stile and then a bit further on a small footbridge and emerge into a field. Keep to the left and at the end go through a gate on your left onto a road; turn right.

4. At the crossroads turn right again (signposted to Water), and you will see the Kestor Inn on your left as you do so. At the T-junction turn left (signposted to the Bovey valley, Lustleigh and Manaton (indirect)). The lane curves to the right, passing a beautiful row of thatched granite cottages as it does so. You will come to a gate; turn left, following the bridlepath sign and continuing on the path round a house. At the junction, go straight on (signposted to the Bovey valley for Lustleigh).

Bear right just before the next gate to follow a narrow track between banks, and at the junction go left, following the bridlepath sign. Be careful as it is rather wet and rough along here. You go through a gate and the path winds along the edge of a wood and then starts to descend steeply into the valley. When you come to a path going off to the right, carry straight on (signposted to Clam Bridge and Lustleigh Cleave). The path descends even more steeply and you can hear – and soon see – the River Bovey flowing noisily below you.

5. When you come to the bottom of the valley, do not cross the footbridge, but turn right (signposted to the Manaton old road for Trendlebere Down).

The path follows the river fairly closely for about a mile, and then turns sharp right away from it. You now meet up with the Becka Brook again. Follow it upstream for a short distance and then turn left to cross a stile and bridge, and rejoin the track you started out on. Turn left and follow the track back up to Trendlebere Down. Near the top, you will find the path running off to the right to the parking area.

PLACES OF INTEREST

The *Riverside Centre* at Bovey Tracey is the headquarters of the Devon Guild of Craftsmen, and has beautiful exhibitions of the work of the Guild's members. Also at Bovey Tracey is the *Cardew Teapottery*, where you can see novelty teapots being made, and the *House of Marbles*, which has demonstrations of glassblowing. At Newton Abbot, 6 miles beyond Bovey Tracey, *Tucker's Maltings* is a working malthouse which offers guided tours.

WALK 16
THE TAVY AND THE WALKHAM

This is a varied route with much to interest both the natural historian and the social historian. It takes in two delightfully wooded river valleys, stretches of open moorland, farm fields and quiet, often flower-filled lanes and tracks. And in addition to the varied flora, you can see some of the remains of West Devon's industrial past along the way. It is mostly fairly undemanding, but there is one long, steep climb to negotiate.

Buckland Monachorum – the start of the walk.

The valley of the River Tavy was once a rich copper-mining area; indeed, in the 1860s over half the world's copper came from Devon, much of it from this area. As you wander through the beautiful, peaceful woods that now flank both the Tavy and its tributary the Walkham, it is difficult to imagine the activity that must have gone on here during the mines' heyday, when they employed over 1,300 people. Some of the ruins and spoil heaps can still be seen, including the Virtuous Lady Mine (which is presumed to have been named after Elizabeth I) near the confluence of the Tavy and the Walkham, and a solitary engine-house chimney with the remains of associated buildings further up the Walkham.

The walk starts in the picturesque village of Buckland Monachorum. The name means the 'book land' (land held by royal charter) of the monks, the monks referred to being those of nearby Buckland Abbey, which was founded in the 13th century. The main street, with its stone houses, imposing church and attractive pub, is a delight. The pub, the Drake Manor Inn (telephone: 01822 853892), takes its name from Sir Francis Drake, who made his home at Buckland Abbey. It is an unpretentious but very pleasant hostelry which offers a good range of food and drink both at midday and in the evenings.

The route then takes you along farm paths and lanes to the banks of the River Tavy and follows the river upstream before veering away to climb up to the edge of Dartmoor. After a stretch of open moorland, you descend to the river again, and follow it and then its tributary the Walkham through a delightful wood, passing the remains of the mining activity from time to time. After a steep climb back up to the bracken-covered moor, a pretty lane edged with flowers in season takes you back to Buckland Monachorum.

- **HOW TO GET THERE:** Turn west off the A386 Plymouth to Tavistock road just south of Yelverton and follow the signs to Buckland Monachorum. Just beyond the village sign, turn right to reach the village centre.
- **PARKING:** The church car park is on the left as you go towards the village centre. You are requested not to park there during or just before church services (the times are given at the car park entrance). There is also a limited amount of parking in the road, but do be careful not to block any entrances.
- **LENGTH OF THE WALK:** 5$^1/_2$ miles. Maps: OS Landranger 201 Plymouth and Launceston; OS Explorer 108 Lower Tamar Valley and Plymouth (GR 489683).

THE WALK

1. Walk down to the village centre, and immediately beyond the post office and stores turn left down a path. There is a public footpath sign, but it is on the post office wall, and is therefore not visible from this direction. This takes you between some buildings

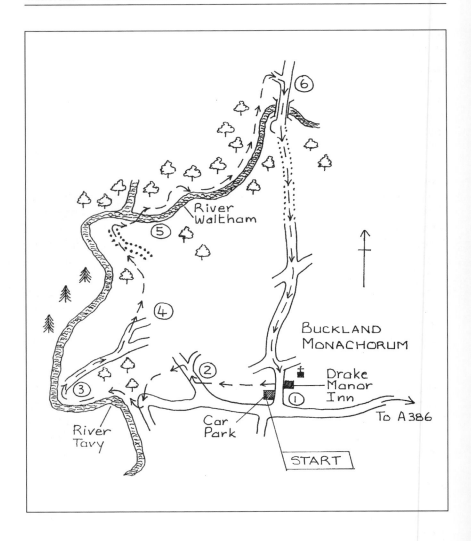

and through a gate to a road on a modern housing estate. Carry straight on along the road, past a school playing field, and at the end go straight on to the right of a house, following a public footpath sign, to a stile.

Keep to the left of the field beyond, and at the path junction go straight on to another stile. Keep to the left again to yet another stile, which leads onto a track. Follow the track to a gate and keep to the right of the field on the other side to another gate. Keep to the right of the next field and where the hedge takes a bend to the right go straight on to a stile, which leads down some steps into a lane.

2. Turn right, and at the junction about 100 yards along the lane turn left up a drive, following the public footpath sign. This climbs into a wood. At the top, where the drive curves to the right, bear off left alongside the bank, following the footpath sign. You eventually come to a stile; keep to the left of the field beyond it and cross a stone stile at the end.

Follow the path on the other side, alongside a bank on your left. Soon you will come to a very steep, wooded slope down to a stream on your right. Cross another stile and you will come out at a lane, where it takes a very sharp bend. Carry straight on, following the lane downhill. After about 75 yards, turn sharp right along a drive, following the public footpath sign.

This takes you down through a gateway towards a house; carry straight on past the entrance to the house, and where the drive turns right towards some outhouses go straight on again along a grassy track which leads you into a wood. The track narrows to a path and soon meets up with the river.

You pass a fallen tree and the path goes over some rocks alongside the river; take care along here as the rocks can become slippery. Cross a stile by a weir and continue along the bank. After the weir, the river flows rather more placidly and it is beautifully peaceful in the wood. Go through a gap in a fence and along a broad path slightly away from the river. At the end, a gate leads into a farmyard; follow the track on the other side to reach a gate onto a surfaced lane.

3. Follow the lane as it climbs steadily out of the valley. At the top it levels out and meets another lane at a T-junction; turn left (signposted to Coppicetown). After about 100 yards, as the lane goes to the right, go straight on up a track. The track soon narrows to a path, which continues to climb until you come to a gate leading onto bracken-covered moorland.

4. You will be faced with a choice of three broad paths through the bracken: one bears right, one bears left and one goes sharp left. Take the one that bears left. It soon joins another coming in from

The remains of a copper mine beside the River Walkham.

the right. You get a lovely view across the densely wooded Tavy valley from up here.

Where the path forks, go left. You descend gradually to join a track; bear left again, and continue to descend. Here gorse and heather are added to the bracken. The track goes to the right of a cottage; follow it as it twists and turns down to the river. This is where the Virtuous Lady Mine was. You will find a path going off to the left; take it to go down to the riverbank.

Follow the river upstream and you will soon come to its confluence with the Walkham. Follow the Walkham upstream for a few yards to a footbridge.

5. Cross the bridge and follow the path along the bank of the Tavy for a few yards before turning off onto a new path between two large outcrops of rock. This will take you down to a lovely clear area and up the right bank of the River Walkham. After a while the path leaves the water to climb up the side of the valley. Cross a track and continue to climb up the hill to join it higher up. Turn right.

Pass a house on your right and follow the track as it narrows to a path and rejoins the river. It is delightful along here, with the wood clinging to the hill on your left, the river bubbling and swirling on your right and the light filtering through the trees and dappling the water. You pass an old engine-house chimney and 500 yards beyond that go through a gate and bear left around a house. The path comes out at a lane; bear left.

6. At the T-junction turn right. Cross the river and a cattle grid, and go straight on along a track, past a car park. Ignore the path to the left just beyond the car park and the broad area to the right just beyond that; just follow the track as it climbs through the wood, twisting and turning as it does so. It is a steep climb; take it gently, as it is also a long one.

At the top it emerges onto open moorland again, and you get another lovely view across the Tavy valley to the right. Ignore the paths that lead off to the left and right and follow the track straight across the moorland to a parking area. Cross a cattle grid just beyond it and follow the lane on the other side.

At the crossroads, go straight on (signposted to Buckland Monachorum). A little more than $1/2$ mile beyond that you will

The River Tavy

come to a T-junction; turn left (signposted to Crapstone). At the next junction follow the main lane round to the right (signposted to Crapstone again), and it will take you back to the centre of the village.

PLACES OF INTEREST

Just a few hundred yards from the centre of Buckland Monachorum is the *Garden House*, a ruined 16th-century vicarage surrounded by 8 acres of beautiful gardens, while about a mile away is *Buckland Abbey*, now in the hands of the National Trust. In Yelverton, 1½ miles away, there is the interesting *Paperweight Centre*.

DARTMOOR: THE UPPER MEAVY
AND THE DEVONPORT LEAT

Here you have the opportunity to enjoy the full splendour of Dartmoor as you follow the River Meavy down to Burrator Reservoir and then cut up to join the Devonport Leat as it meanders across the open moor. The tranquillity of the wide open spaces soothes the spirit, while the grandeur of the tors and the views take the breath away. There is also much of historical interest to see along the way. The going is generally fairly easy, although the ground can become boggy in places.

The Devonport Leat.

The Devonport Leat was constructed at the end of the 18th century and the beginning of the 19th to bring water to the expanding dock area of Devonport, now part of Plymouth. It was a major undertaking; it drew its water from the West Dart and Cowsic rivers and took it 27 miles to Devonport, contouring round the hills and tors of Dartmoor for most of its length. Much of it is still in use, although it now empties into Burrator Reservoir.

Your route takes you down the valley of the River Meavy, from its source near Princetown to the plantations around Burrator Reservoir. On the way you pass through the workings of some of the medieval tinners, who panned for ore in the river and threw up mounds of spoil along the bank. When the ore in the river was exhausted, they dug into the hillside, creating deep gullies known as girts, and there are examples of these to see as you go as well. You also cross the Devonport Leat where it cascades down from the hillside to go over the river via an aqueduct.

From the reservoir you return to the open moor to rejoin the leat and follow it upstream for about a mile, passing a couple of interesting crosses along the way. These mark the route of an ancient transmoor track, known as the Monks' Path, which was used by monks travelling between the abbeys at Buckfast and Tavistock. There are superb views here, as there are on the final leg, which leaves the leat and cuts straight across the moor to Princetown.

Princetown is home to Dartmoor high security prison, and its granite bulk dominates the village. It was originally built at the beginning of the 19th century to house French prisoners from the Napoleonic Wars, as well as Americans captured during the Anglo-American war of 1812.

Our route passes the High Moorland Visitor Centre in Princetown, which is worth a visit. It has some excellent displays and exhibits of the history, geology and flora and fauna of the moor. And for refreshments, I can strongly recommend the Plume of Feathers (telephone: 01822 890240). It is a delightful 18th-century pub which serves coffee and tea as well as a wide variety of drinks and freshly prepared food which ranges from toasted sandwiches to main meals, including their monster grill.

- **HOW TO GET THERE:** The B3212 from Yelverton to Moretonhampstead passes through Princetown.
- **PARKING:** There is a car park behind the High Moorland Visitor Centre; follow the signs.
- **LENGTH OF THE WALK:** 7^1/$_2$ miles. Maps: OS Landranger 191 Okehampton and North Dartmoor (start and finish), 202 Torbay and South Dartmoor (middle section); OS Outdoor Leisure 28 Dartmoor (GR 590735).

The Devonport Leat tumbling down Raddick Hill.

THE WALK

1. Follow the path past the toilets and round in front of the High Moorland Visitor Centre. You will see the Plume of Feathers straight ahead of you, across the main road. Turn right and follow the road out of the village. Just outside the village you cross a cattle grid. You are now on the open moor, and as you come over the brow of a hill, a beautiful view comes into sight, across a series of tors to the farmland of West Devon and Cornwall beyond. The track you can see on your right is the route of the Plymouth and Dartmoor Railway, which was built towards the beginning of the 19th century in an attempt to open up this part of Dartmoor for development, and which finally closed in 1956.

2. After about $1/2$ mile the road curves to the right and goes down into a dip. To the right in the dip is a marshy area which marks the start of the River Meavy; go left to follow the river (at this stage no more than a stream) as it emerges from under the road. The area alongside the river can be very boggy, so it is probably best to walk along the top of the bank above it, keeping to the left of the river. As you go, you will see the mounds formed by the spoil thrown up by the early tinners as they streamed for ore in the river bed.

As you follow the valley down, you can appreciate the quiet and sense of space that is a feature of the moor; on some days, your only companions may be the sheep and the crows. The going can be a bit rough in places, with the grass growing in tussocks and the occasional marshy stretch, but there are plenty of paths to guide you through. You will pass the remains of more tin workings, formed as the miners dug into the hillside in their search for ore. It is not necessary to keep too close to the river, as long as you follow the line of the valley.

Soon you will see the aqueduct carrying the Devonport Leat across the river ahead of you. Before you reach it you will have to cross the Hart Tor Brook, which comes down from your left. Probably the best place to do this is where it joins the Meavy and is channelled into a sluice, although there are stepping stones higher up which are perfectly passable if the brook is not too high.

3. When you reach the aqueduct, climb left up the bank to cross the Devonport Leat at a sluice. Once across, make your way back to the aqueduct and go down a steep bank to continue along the river. (If you try to take what looks like the easy route straight on from the

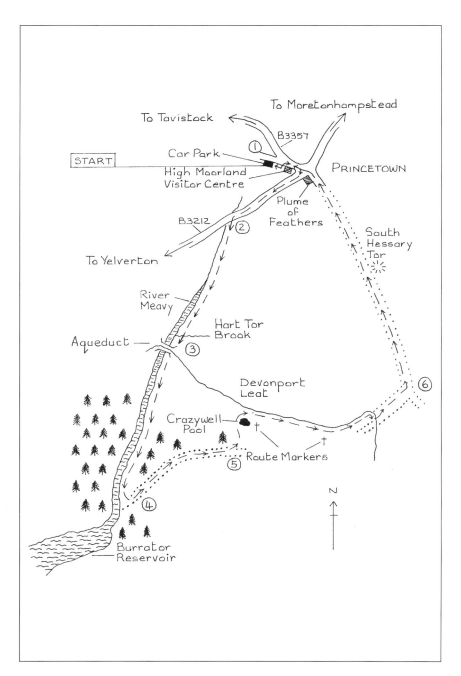

sluice, you will find yourself crossing a very wet patch.) The path alongside the river winds through some more extensive tin workings.

Where the river enters a plantation, go across a stile onto a track (signposted to Leather Tor Bridge). Follow the track as it curves slightly away from the river, and soon the latter will be hidden by the trees on your right, although you will still be able to hear it. After a while, however, the track meets up with it again and runs alongside it. You pass a track coming down from the left and then come to a junction in the path, with a bridge on your right. Go straight on (signposted to Norsworthy Bridge). This is a particularly pretty stretch, with the river cascading down through the trees below you on your right.

4. You come to a T-junction; turn left (signposted 'County road Raddick Lane'). This track climbs and twists, with the plantation on your left and open country on the right. Towards the top of the climb, look back for a good view over Burrator Reservoir. Where the plantation finally ends, you go through a gateway and continue along the track on the other side.

5. About 400 yards beyond the gate, you will see a deep gully running up on your left. This is a girt, and was formed by the activities of the tin miners. Leave the track and follow the line of the girt up the hill. After a couple of hundred yards you will come to Crazywell Pool, an old mine working which has filled with water. Go past it and continue up the hill, and after about 150 yards you will come to the Devonport Leat again.

Turn right and follow the bank of the leat. After a while, you will see a cross on your right, and then about 1/2 mile further on, another one. These mark the route of the Monks' Path, which ran between Buckfast Abbey to the east of the moor and Tavistock Abbey to the west. Follow the leat until it bends round to the right and then crosses a track. Turn left onto the track and continue for about 500 yards.

6. When you come to a junction; turn left. You get a superb view half right across the moor as you do so, and also a good view over to the farms of West Devon to the left. After a little over 3/4 mile you pass South Hessary Tor on the right, and about 1/2 mile beyond that

One of the impressive route markers for the Monks' Path.

you come to a gate. Go through and you will see Princetown below you, with the gloomy bulk of Dartmoor Prison glowering over the village on the other side. Follow the track down to another gate and onto a path, which leads to a road. At the crossroads go straight on across the main road and bear left round the High Moorland Visitor Centre to return to the car park.

PLACES OF INTEREST

In Princetown itself, the *High Moorland Visitor Centre* will give you an excellent introduction to Dartmoor and its people. The *Paperweight Centre* at Yelverton, 6 miles away, has an unusual collection of over 800 paperweights. Further west, near Buckland Monachorum (8 miles), the *Garden House* has superb gardens, while about a mile beyond that is the National Trust property of *Buckland Abbey*, once the home of Sir Francis Drake.

THE PLYM AND THE LOWER MEAVY

Open moorland and cool green woods, steep-sided valleys and fertile farm fields – variety is the keynote of this delightful route. And for added interest it visits an Iron Age settlement and the Dewerstone – according to legend the Devil's place of execution, but now a popular rock-climbing venue. And once you have negotiated the long but steady climb near the beginning of the walk, it is all easy going.

The Skylark Inn in the village of Clearbrook.

At their confluence, both the Plym and Meavy rivers tumble and cascade over a series of rapids and large boulders through wooded valleys. The steep hillsides on either side are also strewn with boulders, and the moss-covered trees seem at times to grow straight out of the rocks, lending the woods a somewhat eerie beauty.

It is not surprising, therefore, that one of the massive rocks jutting out from the woods above the Plym has been associated with the Devil and given the name the Dewerstone – Old Dewer being one

111

of the names by which he was known in these parts. It was said that he sallied forth at night from Wistman's Wood, near Two Bridges, with his pack of hounds – known as the Wisht Hounds – on the hunt for souls. He then chased his victims to the Dewerstone, where he left them to fall to their deaths in the valley below.

Just above the Dewerstone, on the promontory formed by the two valleys, are the remains of a Bronze Age settlement and a later Iron Age hillfort. They have not stood up to the ravages of time as well as many of the other sites on Dartmoor, but there are still the remains of one or two walls to be seen.

The route to the Plym valley takes you from the little one-street village of Clearbrook up onto the open moorland of Wigford Down and then down through Dewerstone Wood past the dreaded stone itself – now very popular with the rock-climbing fraternity. On the way back you have a chance to experience the different moods of the Meavy, first a raging torrent cascading and tumbling over boulders in a steep-sided valley then a quiet, tranquil river flowing placidly between farm fields as you return to Clearbrook.

Clearbrook itself is an attractive little village of whitewashed, slate-roofed cottages, formerly a mining settlement. The Skylark Inn (telephone: 01822 853258) is an 18th-century farmhouse which was converted to serve the needs of the thirsty miners and now offers a mouthwatering array of meals, from the usual bar snacks to full meals and daily specials.

- **HOW TO GET THERE:** Clearbrook is signposted east off the A386 Plymouth to Tavistock road just north of Plymouth.
- **PARKING:** There is a small pull-in on the right just beyond the village, and you can usually also find parking in the village street.
- **LENGTH OF THE WALK:** $4^1/_2$ miles. Maps: OS Landranger 201 Plymouth and Launceston; OS Outdoor Leisure 28 Dartmoor (GR 522656).

THE WALK

1. Take the lane east from Clearbrook and follow it down the hill, across a cattle grid and under an old railway bridge. You pass some cottages on the right and then cross the River Meavy. Just beyond the bridge you come to a junction; go straight on (signposted to Cadover Bridge). The lane climbs out of the valley among some trees and alongside a stream. It is a long hill, so take it steadily. You

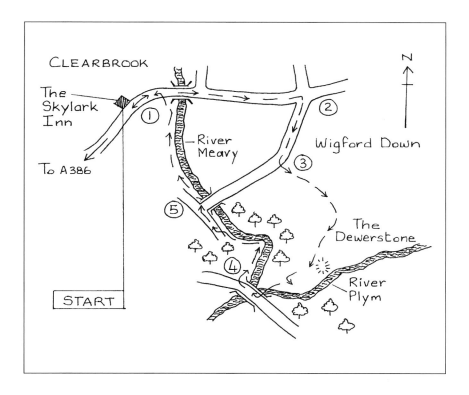

cross a cattle grid, and continue to climb until you come out onto the open moorland and reach a crossroads, where you get an excellent view of the moors ahead of you.

2. Turn right (signposted to Goodameavy) and follow the road down into a dip and up the other side. You pass some houses, and as you do so you get a very good view over Plymouth.

3. About ¹/₂ mile beyond the crossroads you will see a stone cross on the left, with a wall behind it. Turn off the road here and follow the wall up onto Wigford Down, crossing a rivulet as you go. When the wall takes a sharp turn to the right, go half right, aiming to the left of the rocks you can see on the horizon. As you come up alongside them, you again get an excellent view ahead down the valley to Plymouth and beyond. This is the site of the prehistoric settlement and hillfort.

The River Plym from Shaugh Bridge.

Cross a wall and follow a path straight down towards a pile of rocks below you, keeping to the right of them. Go on down, keeping to the right of the next rock, and you will find a path running right, and the Dewerstone below you on the left. Turn right and follow the path along the side of the hill. Soon it becomes more definite and is paved.

After a short distance you come to a junction. Turn sharp left along the paved path, which soon turns sharply to the right again and takes you down alongside the Plym and then round to the left to cross a wooden footbridge. On the other side, turn right to go down to a road. Turn right again to cross Shaugh Bridge, which spans the confluence of the two rivers.

4. Immediately across the bridge, turn right off the road along an unsignposted path. This closely follows the bank of the Meavy through Knowle Wood. This is a lovely stretch, with the river tumbling noisily over the rocks on your right, and the wood stretching up the boulder-strewn hillside on your left.

Just over ³/₄ mile after leaving Shaugh Bridge, the path forks, with the more obvious route going to the left up a bank. Follow it up and you will find yourself walking alongside a dried-up leat. It soon passes under the track of a disused railway line, and the path joins the track. Bear right and follow the track until you see a gap in the fence on your left, with a large notice indicating that you are on the Plym Valley Cycleway. Go through the gap into a lane and turn right.

5. After about 50 yards you will come to a road running off to the right, signposted to Goodameavy. Turn down it, passing under a railway bridge, and after a few yards go left across a stile, following the footpath sign. Cross a small field to a wooded area. On the other side, cross another field, cutting off a bend in the river, to three stiles in quick succession, followed by another wooded area. The path soon runs alongside the dry course of the leat again, with the embankment of the disused railway up to your left.

Cross a stile into a field, and keep alongside the river as you cross it. The river is a lot more sedate along here than lower down its course, and this is a lovely, peaceful stretch, with trees lining the bank. At the end of the field, climb a ladder stile to a road. Turn left, away from the river, and climb the short hill back to Clearbrook.

PLACES OF INTEREST

The *Paperweight Centre* at Yelverton, 3 miles to the north of Clearbrook, has an unusual collection of paperweights. Near Buckland Monachorum (5 miles) are the *Garden House*, with a beautiful garden, and *Buckland Abbey*, a National Trust property which was the home of Sir Francis Drake.

WALK 19

THE RIVER AVON AND BIGBURY BAY

There are some lovely views for you to savour on this delightful ramble down the Avon estuary and along the South Hams coast. The birdlife is also interesting and varied, and the villages through which you pass are enchanting. There is one steady climb towards the middle of the walk, but otherwise the going is relatively easy.

The beach at Thurlestone.

The South Hams, the peninsula south of Totnes and Brixham, is a beautiful part of Devon, and the area around Bigbury Bay is particularly lovely – and extremely varied in its attractions. There is, of course, the rugged coastline, with the waves pounding on rocks below high cliffs, but further inland there are pretty villages of whitewashed thatched cottages, rich, rolling farmland and cool, green woods. And the River Avon, slow and majestic at this point, provides a haven for a variety of waterbirds, from the ubiquitous gulls to mallards and herons.

Your route starts in the pretty village of Bantham and follows the Avon estuary to the coast. You then take the South Devon Coast Path along the cliff-top, with lovely views along Bigbury Bay, to Thurlestone. Here you turn inland and wander through this long, attractive village and down to the equally attractive hamlet of West Buckland.

A climb through a lane bounded by high hedges is followed by a delightful green lane, full of flowers in season and wildlife, which meanders past fields and meadows. The final stretch takes you through a pretty wood and across fields to follow the Avon as it makes its way down to Bantham and the sea.

There are two pubs along the way, and both can be recommended. The Sloop Inn at Bantham (telephone: 01548 560489), near the start of the walk, is a very attractive village pub with a friendly atmosphere which offers a wide selection of bar meals and snacks, with seafood as a speciality. And almost halfway round, at Thurlestone, you will find the Thurlestone Hotel with its Village Inn pub (telephone: 01548 560382). The hotel itself is a somewhat grander establishment – although very friendly nonetheless – but the pub has a very relaxed atmosphere. Here you can get light lunches, coffees and cream teas.

- **HOW TO GET THERE:** Bantham is clearly signposted off the A379 Kingsbridge to Plymouth road near Churchstow.
- **PARKING:** There is a car park at the end of the village.
- **LENGTH OF THE WALK:** 4^1/$_2$ miles. Maps: OS Landranger 202 Torbay and South Dartmoor; OS Outdoor Leisure 20 South Devon (GR 667437).

THE WALK

1. Follow the track that leaves the car park at the opposite end from the village. At the fork go left, and at the end of the track cross a stile on your left and turn right along the edge of a field. As you go, you get a good view of Burgh Island ahead of you, Bigbury-on-Sea across the estuary and the long stretch of coast beyond.

Follow the path round to the left along the cliff. There is a bit of a climb, and at the top you cross a stile and continue along the edge of the cliff on the other side, still climbing. Soon the path levels off

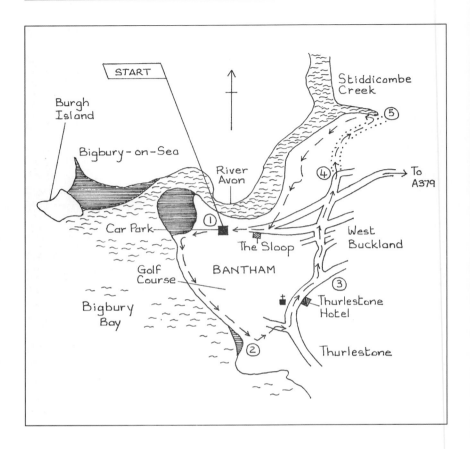

and you get another grand view, this time across Bigbury Bay ahead of you.

At the path junction, go straight on. The path skirts Thurlestone golf course, with a steep slope down to the rocks on the right. There are flowers all around in season, and the birds are prolific, with gulls everywhere and cormorants drying themselves on the rocks below. At the next path junction, go straight on again, keeping an eye open for golf balls.

2. You will soon see a cove with a beach ahead of you. About halfway round it you will come to a path leading left, across the golf course; take it, watching out for golf balls again. On the other side of the golf course, go through a gate on your left leading to a path.

Some of the attractive homes in Thurlestone.

At the end, turn right into a road, and at the T-junction turn left. You are now on the main road through Thurlestone. It is a long village, but keep to the main road, passing the war memorial and then the church on your left as you go. Just beyond the church, you will find the Thurlestone Hotel on your right, with the Village Inn alongside the main hotel. Beyond the hotel, you come to the old part of the village, a particularly attractive collection of thatched cottages.

3. About 250 yards from the hotel, turn left up a side lane (signposted to Bantham and Buckland). It takes you up a hill and out of the village. As you come over the brow of the hill, you get a very good view ahead over the undulating farmland. You then descend somewhat steeply; at the junction at the bottom, follow the main lane round to the left (signposted to Bantham).

The lane climbs up the side of the valley, through the pretty hamlet of West Buckland. Go straight across the first junction (signposted to Bantham), and at the next, where Bantham is signposted to the left and Kingsbridge to the right, go straight across again. The lane continues to climb steadily for some time, so take it gently. At the crossroads at the top of the hill, go straight across again. You now get another lovely view ahead over the rolling fields, and through the gaps in the hedge on your left you can see down the River Avon to Burgh Island.

At the end of the lane, where it goes round to the right to a house, go straight on along a track bounded by high hedges. The wild flowers are particularly prolific along here, and the track winds gently down between the fields towards the river valley. About 1/2 mile along the track, you will find a gate blocking it; a few yards before you reach it, turn left through another gate, following the direction of the yellow arrow. Bear right in the field beyond, to go down towards the head of Stiddicombe Creek, which you can see below you.

4. When you reach the bottom, turn left. You enter a pretty wood and follow the path through it, with the creek on your right. You should see the birds on and around the water as you go. After a while, as the creek joins the river, you will have to climb up through the wood to avoid fallen trees.

You emerge from the wood and go along the top of the field beyond, with a good view across the river on your right. Cross a stile and keep to the top of the next field to another stile. At the end of the third field, the path goes round to the left to a gate. Cross a track to another gate and bear right. Cross a footbridge and climb a hill to a stile followed by some steps leading up to a track; bear right. You still get a good view across the Avon and you will soon see Burgh Island half right as the river takes a broad sweep to the right.

Go through a gate and continue along the track at the top of the next field. After another gate, the track leaves the farmland and runs beside some houses into Bantham. It emerges through yet another gate onto a lane; turn right and follow the lane past the Sloop Inn to the car park.

PLACES OF INTEREST

Just north of Kingsbridge, about 6 miles from Bantham, is the *Sorley Tunnel Adventure Farm*, an attractive farm park with craft workshops. And at Modbury, a little over 9 miles away, north-west along the A379, you can visit the *Woodturner's Craft Centre* and see wood turners and carvers at work.

HALLSANDS AND START POINT

This walk offers stunning coastal views for very little effort, taking you almost to the southernmost tip of Devon, and passing a ruined fishing village with an interesting history on the way back.

Great Mattiscombe Sand.

The flourishing fishing village of Hallsands stood on the rocky shore of Start Bay for some 300 years, but sadly succumbed to the elements in 1917, being washed away by violent storms in January of that year. The ruins can still be seen, a poignant reminder of the power of the sea, but they can no longer be visited, as the cliff has subsided. Efforts are being made to shore it up, but at the time of writing it looks as though it will be some time before it will be safe to venture down to the old village again – if it ever is.

The modern village is actually two hamlets, North and South Hallsands, connected only by the Coast Path; driving between the two involves a detour inland. North Hallsands consists of a small cluster of houses stretching down to the beach and the Hallsands Hotel, and South Hallsands, which is just above the ruins of the old village, centres around Trouts Tearoom and holiday apartments. The tearoom (telephone: 01548 511296) is a delightful place to stop for refreshments. It has a garden on the cliff top and is licensed. The Hallsands Hotel (telephone: 01548 511264) offers a warm welcome and serves soups, ploughman's lunches, toasted sandwiches and a range of main meals, as well as ice creams and soft drinks. To reach the bar, incidentally, you should go round to the left of the hotel; the front door is sometimes locked.

This walk starts at North Hallsands because that is where the public car park is – the only public parking in South Hallsands is reserved for customers of the tearoom. It follows the path along the coast to South Hallsands, then cuts inland through narrow lanes before following a farm path down to the sea at Great Mattiscombe Sand, with a good view along the coast to Prawle Point.

The South Devon Coast Path takes you across the 'waist' of Start Point, with the option of going to the lighthouse at the end of the headland. From the northern side of Start Point you get a stunning view along the length of Start Bay, past the magnificent Slapton Sands to the Dart and beyond, a view which stays with you as you follow the Coast Path back to Hallsands, passing the ruins of the old village along the way.

- **HOW TO GET THERE:** Turn south off the A379 Kingsbridge to Dartmouth road at Stokenham, and follow the signs to Hallsands and Start Point. About 2 miles from the turn-off you will see a sign pointing left to North Hallsands; turn here to reach the public car park. For South Hallsands, carry on a bit further and you will see the sign, again pointing left.
- **PARKING:** The public car park is at North Hallsands. There is a car park at South Hallsands, but it is reserved for customers of Trouts Tearoom. If you are planning to visit the tearoom, the proprietors may be prepared to let you leave your car there while you walk. On the other hand, if they are very busy they may not be too happy about it; and if they object, it is quite a long detour back to North Hallsands, which is the nearest public parking.
- **LENGTH OF THE WALK:** 3¾ miles. Maps: OS Landranger 202 Torbay and South Dartmoor; OS Outdoor Leisure 20 South Devon (GR 817388).

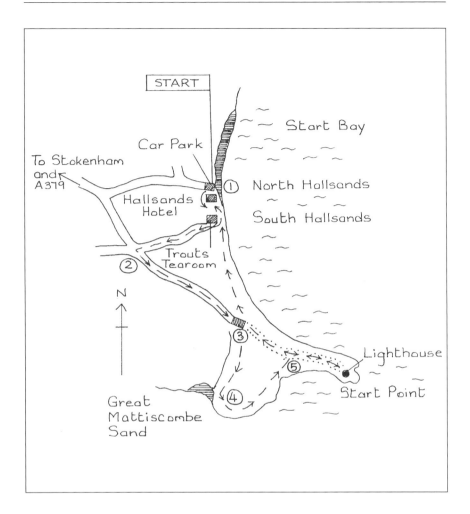

THE WALK

1. Follow the road to the Hallsands Hotel, and then take the Coast Path, which is signposted round to the right. Climb some steep steps alongside the hotel. At the top you get a superb view along the coast to Start Point, as the path passes in front of some houses to Trouts. Turn right down a lane just beyond the tearoom and follow it past some tennis courts and a putting green. Once out of the village, it climbs steadily up a valley and curves to the right. At the junction, follow the main lane round to the left.

2. At the crossroads, turn left (signposted to Start Point). The lane is bounded by high hedges for most of the time, but you do get the occasional view over the fields to the coast on your left. It is a pleasant, easy stroll, and the hedgerows are full of interest. You soon pass a radio transmission station on your right and the lane curves to the right and begins to descend gradually. You pass Start Farm, also on the right, and finally come to a car park. Cross it and bear right at the end to join the Coast Path and cross a stile.

3. Immediately on the other side, turn right (signposted to Great Mattiscombe Sand) and go through a gate. Follow the path on the other side between fields. It soon bears left to follow the valley of a small stream downhill, and you get a good view down to the coast and out to sea.

4. Near the bottom, the path emerges through a gate just above Great Mattiscombe Sand, and you meet the Coast Path. Go straight on towards the sea, rather than following the right-hand route, which skirts the beach and heads west. At the end, follow the path round to the left, just above the sea and the rocks.

You will soon begin to climb among some large outcrops on your left as you round the headland. Take care along here, as the path becomes somewhat narrow and rocky. Once round, you climb gently up to the top of the cliff, with a good view of Start Point and its lighthouse ahead of you; the rocks below are usually covered by gulls and cormorants. After a while the path swings left and climbs across the 'waist' of Start Point. Pause when you get to the top of the climb, as the view ahead along Start Bay will take your breath away – mile upon mile of beaches (Slapton Sands alone is 3 miles long), followed by small coves and the Dart estuary.

5. On the other side you will meet a surfaced track. Turn right if you want to visit the lighthouse at Start Point, $1/4$ mile away. It is not open to the public – indeed, for safety reasons one can only approach to within about 100-200 yards of it – but it is quite an impressive structure. If you are not visiting it, turn left.

After $1/4$ mile or so, the track will bring you to the car park you passed through on the way out. Keep to the right through it, following the Coast Path along the cliff. You will have that magnificent view along the bay to keep you company all the way;

Start Point lighthouse.

the path is also fringed with a lovely variety of wild flowers in season. After about 700 yards or so, you enter a small wood; as you emerge from it, keep an eye open for the ruined village on the rocks below and ahead of you; it is almost immediately below Trouts. You cross a stile and emerge at Trouts; follow the path on along the coast and down the steps by the hotel to reach the car park.

PLACES OF INTEREST
Slapton Ley Nature Reserve is just 5 miles to the north, and there is a bird hide at the Torcross end where you can watch the multitude of birds on the Ley without disturbing them. *Stancombe Cyder Press*, about 6 miles away at Sherford, off the A379 east of Kingsbridge, offers the chance to see cider being made.